Just Us

Charlie Summers

authorHOUSE®

AuthorHouse™ UK Ltd.
500 Avebury Boulevard
Central Milton Keynes, MK9 2BE
www.authorhouse.co.uk
Phone: 08001974150

First published by AuthorHouse 11/2/2010

ISBN: 978-1-4520-7745-1 (sc)

This book is printed on acid-free paper.

Distant history tremble,
Emotional viewings crumble,
Your words soak into my acts,
Silence doesn't kill any facts,
You sow up my seam,
Under the same stars we dream.....

Contents

Strange Beginnings
Chapter 1

This was it, this was the moment he had dreamed about for what seemed to be an eternity. He was standing there somewhat in the middle of a small arrival gate with his suitcase beside him and his guitar too. God that thing travels everywhere with him. Taking notice of his watch wondering how much longer he would have to wait. As he glanced upwards, it seemed as if the whole world suddenly started to slow down. There were these big windows at the front of the room reaching up as high as the ceiling, only broken by the grey tiled pillars between them. Then, there she was, as if in slow motion walking past one window and then the next getting closer to the revolving doors. Her long brown wavy hair was blowing in the wind. She looked amazing, much more than he could have ever imagined. He dropped his things as she ran to him, throwing her arms around him. Pulling back slightly after a long hug, they look deep into each other's eyes and kiss. He had been travelling for almost thirteen hours now; well it's a long way from Ireland to Canada, but standing there with Nicky finally in his arms made everything worthwhile. Richard had left Ireland, his family, his friends, his job, his car and even his daughter on the hope that he had found true love with a girl he had never met face to face before. Yea I know what you're thinking, probably the same as his friends at the time. That he must be crazy and stupid, and yes maybe he was a little crazy but to explain, I must tell you the whole story, not just from when he first laid eyes on her.

It was early November the previous year and was after ten o'clock when Richard sat down at his computer and found himself logging onto a chat room as he would generally do to pass time. He always found them a good place to have a laugh, talk serious or talk dirty to girls, it was all a bit of a laugh really. However he had met his ex-girlfriend through a chat room, her name was Chloe and she had lived in Belfast and he had lived in Dublin, they had only split up in October. She was a great girl who had helped him work through a lot of issues after his marriage break up earlier in the year. He had taken it pretty bad as he could no longer see his daughter each day. You don't meet too many people in your life who just give, and really just want to be there to help you out and don't have any other motives for friendship or relationships. Well maybe Chloe had just enjoyed his company! Anyways he was in the chat room that night and was looking down the names of the people in there and seen a name irishgirl427. It was an international chat room, and it wouldn't be very often that you'd see other Irish people in there. They get talking, the usual hellos. They exchange messenger details and switch to talking on messenger. Next thing, out of the blue, she sends him an invite to see her on webcam. His heart stopped when he seen her, she was so gorgeous, had this beautiful smile and long brown curly hair. Turned out despite her name in the chat room she was actually from Nova Scotia in Canada. Apparently one of her great grandparents was Irish, and so they got talking about Ireland and Richard sent her a couple pictures which he had saved on his computer of Ireland, ones which he had taken on his travels around the country. She said she's planning to come visit Ireland the following year in May after her exams, so she could follow her roots and he replied in his usual cheekiness saying how he'd take her out for a drink or show her around the country a bit if he could get a few days off work, much to his surprise she said that she'd like that. By this time Richard had his webcam on too and they were having a laugh and getting to know each other a bit, she had such a nice smile that when she smiled, he would smile.

It was like that right from the start! He climbed into bed that night with a smile on his face, something was different about this girl, and it was like an instant click. It's very hard to explain how it was, but he laid there thinking about Nicky, he felt like his feet had been swept from underneath him. Over the following weeks they chatted on messenger on occasion and they also started to send each other emails in-between their chats. They'd send each other pictures and music too, and there was one song in particular he kept listening to at the time was called *Green Eyes*, so he emailed it to her on an attachment.

From: Nicky> nicky@mynl.com
Sent: 17 November
To: Rich> richard@mynl.com
Hey what's up?...ok so I have listened to this song here a few times and wow I love it...and as I have said before boy I tend to read into things...just my nature ya know....so here's what's on my mind...well the song is great...and I think ya sent it for a reason...God if I am so off base please let me know..should have asked ya when ya were online I suppose that way I would know and not ramble on and on like a complete fool...but anyways...I have green eyes...is that just a coincidence?...hmmm...sucks when ya send a message and ya have to wait for a response eh....I feel as though I am just talking to myself....ah well....so anyways.....oh boy too many dots ....
....
..........................well even more than that but I should just get on with it here eh....thing is, is that I do enjoy chatting with ya... ok I like ya a lot....it's funny eh how ya meet someone and they are just so wonderful on so many levels....ever think what if sometimes?....maybe I am just going on all strange and that... but maybe not...ok all I really know is boy you make me smile... which I must say is very nice...people around here that know me would tell ya that's quite an accomplishment...as I am not one to smile at anything all that much...and I know this must seem a bit

3

strange to be saying all this cause we have never met before...
but when we speak I like ya all the more every time more and
more...I have not yet figured it out yet for myself...and maybe it's
not something to be understood... all I know is whatever it may
be I like it and would like it to continue...well I hope that made a
bit of sense...and I hope I did not say too much here...ok then get
back to me...night, mwah infinity, Nicky.
From: Rich> richard@mynl.com
Sent: 18 November
To: Nicky> nicky@mynl.com
Hi Nicky,
I'm glad you liked the song, I have been listening to it lately and
yes I did make the connection between your eyes and the song.
And hey I like you a lot too and I'm glad I make you smile lots
and you make me smile a lot too. I don't know what it is between
us but I really enjoy talking to you. Hey my daughter Ria is here
today, you'd like her, she's just learning to walk now and all that
and looks so cute with her little blonde curls ☺ so I think I am
going to go now and take her off to the park but I'll speak to you
tomorrow night after I drop Ria home to her mum Ann. Talk to
you soon xxx

It was Nicky's birthday a few days after on the 22nd
of November. One of her closest friends was her cousin
Thomas; they grew up together as they just lived around the
corner from each other. Thomas was a year younger than
Nicky; he was shorter too with a trendy light brown hair
style. Nicky had been talking with him about how she was
considering getting back with her ex boyfriend David. I
suppose looking at it from her side of things, she and David
had two kids together and David kept on asking her to take
him back, so I guess she was planning just to give it a try for
the kid's sakes. She had a boy Gavin who was four at the
time and Lauren who was turning six in January. Thing is,
Thomas knew some info about David which he had never

4

told Nicky as they were split up now and there was no point. On Nicky's birthday, Thomas took her out for a game of pool down the pub, and they got totally drunk and stoned, and then Thomas told her all he knew about how David had told her so many lies and had been with other women while they had been together. It hit Nicky really the next day once the drugs and alcohol had worked their way out of her system, Nicky and David had been together for seven years in total, which is the same amount if time Richard had been with his ex-wife Ann. It was a couple of nights later when they caught up with each other online and she filled him in with all the details. She was on webcam and he could tell she had been crying. He wanted to be there and to give her a hug and tell her everything would be alright. They talked for hours, and by the time they said goodnight, he had her smiling again.

Things developed quickly into December and what were occasional chats became chats almost every day. Richard got into this routine everyday which was go to work, come home, have dinner and then study for two hours and then either go for a walk or do some exercise, have a shower, and then log on the internet and talk to Nicky till he could not stay awake any longer! There was a four hour time difference between that Nova Scotia and Ireland so he would be on for eleven o'clock which was seven for her. Sometimes they talked until five in the morning, and then he'd grab an hour's sleep and get up for work. It started to kick in then, missing each other when they couldn't make it online, or if the internet connection wasn't working. It started to dawn on both of them that this was more than just a friendship developing, but neither of them understood what they should do, and no one around them seemed to understand what they had. It scared Richard, it scared him a lot! I mean Nicky lived in Canada, has two kids and goes to college and he lived here in Ireland, had a kid too, so how would they ever make this work? Like how could they ever exist in the same place, and have their kids together and everything. They talked about this, and well part of the plan became that when she was coming over in May, that they would spend some time going around a couple of the colleges here in Dublin. I suppose it was the best option for her to move over with the kids, she had more rights to move here with the kids, as Richard knew he could never move with his daughter Ria with him. They left their thoughts wandering around the same idea for the next while and let the thoughts about it pass and they just continued to enjoy each other's company. Richard went away to London for a week to visit his best friend Rachel for her birthday. Rachel was three years younger than him and was as tall as Richard's shoulders; she always wore her hair blonde and straight. It's the first time he had been back over there since his summer trip there after his marriage had fallen apart. He had missed Rachel, and the whole week over there became a big celebration as Rachel was turning 22. However he thought about Nicky while he was away and did miss talking to her.

From: Nicky> nicky@mynl.com
Sent: 12 December
To: Rich> richard@mynl.com
Hey just wanted to send ya a little hello just in case I am not online when ya come on ...I am headed to my dad's for dinner with the kids he wants us to come up and help decorate their tree so I may not be able to get on in time to chat with ya as it may be late when I get back....sorry for that....I hope you had a great weekend and I hope to chat with ya again really soon....if I don't catch up with ya tonight I will definitely be on tomorrow night if ya like.....I have missed seeing ya....mwah infinity...and I hope ya have a great day tomorrow at work....well I am leaving now so I will talk to you soon as I can....have a good night, mwah, mwah, mwah....see ya Nicky.

From: Richard> richard@mynl.com
Sent: 12 December
To: Nicky> nicky@mynl.com
Hey Nicky, that's ok. You go and have fun with the kids around
at your dad's, I know you had lots of fun doing your own tree,
I'm surprised you're not going around all the houses in the town
decorating them haha... Well I think I am just going to relax here
with my brother Stephen and have a few drinks or something, but
I will be online later and I'm normally up late so check when ya
get back, I might still be up and sure if not then I'll catch up with
you tomorrow. Talk to you soon xxx
From: Nicky> nicky@mynl.com
Sent: 15 December
To: Rich> richard@mynl.com
Hey what's up?...just wanted to say I am sorry for going so
quickly last night...my Gran rang me from the hospital and
wanted me to find my mother because she couldn't find her to
tell her the news....my granddad is stabilized now and doing ok...
he is still in the ICU though they think he may have had another
stroke so it's not that good eh....well I am just getting in now I
got the rest of the day off...I am just getting some things taken
care of here before Lauren's Christmas concert at the school....
it's tonight so I don't imagine I will be able to get on in time later...
it's at 6.00pm so I have to be going here I still have a few things
to do here first...well I hope ya had a great day and have yourself
an even better night...I will talk to you soon, mwah, mwah, mwah
infinity as always, I'll be thinking of ya as I do....hugs and many
kisses Nicky.
From: Rich> richard@mynl.com
Sent: 15 December
To: Nicky> nicky@mynl.com
Hey Nicky, yea I wondered where you went last night. I am sorry
to hear your granddad isn't well again, I hope he gets better
soon. I've had a good day here at work and I'm just going to
chill tonight, but yea I hope you have a good time at Lauren's

Christmas concert, I hope you tell me all about it next time we are chatting, maybe even show me some pictures too if you take any?! Anyways I'll catch up with you soon. Miss you xxx talk soon xxx

From: Nicky> nicky@mynl.com
Sent: 18 December
To: Rich> richard@mynl.com

Hey you what's up...I know I am up late aren't I...ah well I just finished watching a really good movie...ya know one of those sappy girly ones that ya laugh and cry at....ya know this is the first time I have been able to bring myself to sit in the living room by myself to watch a movie alone since well when David left.... it wasn't that bad even....may have something to do with me sending this..or maybe not...anyways so I am thinking about a lot of things here and about you...don't be scared it's not my intention...I don't really have a lot to say but I feel like I want to say so much here....this could take a while so if ya don't have time to read it all at once well save it for later and read it then... ya know that I really do like you right?....and I am very happy to have found you...I think that you are so amazing...I would like to say that I am thankful for you helping me through my mess here.. it really means a lot and I just wanted you to know that...you're a wonderful guy...thanks so much ...every day when I think about you and all the what ifs I smile...you make me smile....more than I thought I ever would be able to ...so thanks for that as well.... you make me laugh...and I really like that a lot...and thanks for that ...and I think that if it was possible for us to be together now that well me and you would be so great together.... at any point while you're reading this and start getting all strange just write me back and let me know....I don't mean for ya to feel that way at all...I just want to say what I feel right now and I am scared to death myself...but it's all good right?...I sometimes dream about you...funny cause it's hard for me to see things clearly when I dream it's always a bit fuzzy eh...but all I know is when I wake up after I have had a dream that I feel the same way as when I am talking with ya here...it's a great feeling....and so thanks for that too...never in all my life would I ever had believed to feel this way about someone you have never met was even possible ...but I do and I feel this way about you...and it doesn't go away and nor do I want for it to go away....so what exactly is it that I feel for you is that what you are thinking at this point...I know I have thought this myself....well Richard can I type Richard because I like your name...I feel this great feeling that I am not quite sure I felt before...my heart races... sometimes I don't know what to say when I chat with ya....I get a bit dizzy sometimes....and I like it all I really do...I think I may be falling in love with you...and it's amazing how you can so easily make me feel happy...you make me happy...and I have never met you...have you turned white and passed out yet?....don't because that's not what I meant for ya to do...you can take this anyway ya want but it had to be said and so I said it...scared to pieces but I said it...I don't know what it was or how you have done this but I feel like I am by far the happiest person living right now..if that's possible.....well thanks again for many things...for reading this is another one...well I am going to bed now so I will talk to you soon, mwah infinity as always, thinking of ya..and I hope ya have a great day today and I will try to get on sometime today before I go out to talk with ya....just wouldn't be the same if I didn't....I look forward to it everyday...you're doing a number on me here and I don't mind one bit....I welcome it and want to see where it will go...without fear of anything....so night or good morning to ya....have a good one, hugs kisses and love Nicky x

Unknown to Nicky at the time but Richard had been feeling the exact same way about her, his life only felt complete now with her in it, even though he had never met her before. It may seem weird or strange to you but this is how they felt in their hearts. They had this deep connection, something that went beyond love and sex and everything else. He only knew her since November and she already knew him better than his ex-wife Ann whom he had been with for seven years! They were both interested in psychology and Nicky had been studying it for years and Richard was starting a course for it at the end of January which probably gave them both a bit of an edge to delve deep into each other's heads and figure out how each other's brains ticked along! They never ran out of things to talk about and, well saying goodnight would take longer than the rest of the conversation. Once Richard had read her email and found out how she felt about him, well their next conversation went in one direction. That was it, they made it official, she was his girlfriend and he was her boyfriend. Of course they didn't tell many people, as not one of their friends could even understand, so their relationship became private and very much just between the two of them. But some friends did give them some support even though they didn't understand.

Unfortunately Nicky's granddad didn't get any better and passed away. Richard tried his best to be there for her, on the phone and talking on messenger too. Everyone has some coping mechanism to stress or hurt. Some people use drugs or get drunk, or get violent or go for walks or play music. One thing Richard started to learn at this stage was that Nicky's coping mechanism was going partying at the weekends. This had been the way she faced her problems since she was a teenager, by getting drunk and stoned. However things had started to settle down a bit by Christmas between her and David, and although he would cause hassle when collecting the kids, he did take them for the weekend so that Nicky had some chill out time to herself! Nicky of course due to things that had happened in November used this time to go a little crazy at parties, but she did miss Richard when she was out, as he missed her too when he was out with his friends. Even so much so that when his ex girlfriend Chloe invited him up for a weekend over the Christmas break, he turned her down because he didn't want to be with anyone else except Nicky. Richards coping mechanism for stress and hurt was depression which had haunted him for years since he was young. Nicky wasn't all about the bad experiences in life though. Nicky loved life and especially loved Christmas, therefore they didn't get a huge amount of time to chat over Christmas as she would be off around visiting her mum and her dad and just spending time with Gavin and Lauren while she was off from her studies for a while. Her dad was quite flush with money as he ran his own business and owned a few houses. Over the Christmas break he showed Nicky the details of the trip he was going to pay for her to visit Ireland, and that he might even come with her too. The planned date was 30th of May and this got Richard all excited when Nicky told him. Something to look forward to but also meant a change between Richard and Nicky as they knew now that they would meet for sure, and that it was only a couple of months away, and sure what's a couple of months in the scheme of things?

So here Richard was finally feeling like someone loved him for who he is, and it's a pity she lived thousands of miles away from him. He used to say to Nicky, "God certainly has a sense of humour that he didn't have us born in the same country!" Of course he was being sarcastic!! Richard used to go around with this big chip on the shoulder because he felt life had dealt him such a hard blow, but once he started getting to know Nicky he started to forget his own troubles somehow because she had been through so much in life and had managed to make it through, and trust me his issues were minuscule to hers. Richard felt deeply for her every time she shared that bit more with him about her life, I don't think she had told many people, she tried blocking some stuff from him and everyone. The thing is, is that he came to understand her reactions, all her life men had used and abused her in various ways, and now that Richard began to fall for her and her for him. They both started to become the fairytale romance, you know, the one you think will happen when you're a little naive kid, thinking about love and marriage and kids. Even though both Richard and Nicky had been through the 'settling down' thing before, they found themselves once again becoming a believer in love. They were believers in the fate that they were meant to have met that night in November.

From: Nicky> nicky@mynl.com
Sent: 24 December
To: Rich> richard@mynl.com
Hey what's up? I hope your having a wonderful day....I am just getting ready now to head up to mom's house I am not sure when I will be in or if I will be online later....it may be a little late when I get in here so if you are here when I get back I will talk to you then..If not have a merry Christmas and I will talk to you soon....sorry this is so short here...I have been thinking about ya as I do...smiling....I love ya lots boy, mwah infinity, sweet dreams, night, hugs, kisses and love Nicky
From: Rich> richard@mynl.com
Sent: 24 December
To: Nicky> nicky@mynl.com
Hey gorgeous, how are you doing today? I hope you have a good time up at your mom's house and hope you have a great Christmas there with the kids and all, I bet they are real excited at this point and probably won't get to sleep easily!!?? I miss Ria tonight cause I won't get to see her now till New Year's eve so I'm just trying to keep myself busy here and not think about it. Anyways merry Christmas again xxx miss you xxx

Christmas was a very strange time for Richard. He had moved back in at the parents house after he broke up with Ann. He had spent the last several Christmas's with her. That particular Christmas Richard didn't get to see Ria that much and he didn't get to talk to Nicky much and he didn't get to talk to his best friend Rachel much. It was a bit of a lonesome time, but he got through it alright by looking ahead to the course he would be starting soon. I think part of it was the hope of something new for the start of a new year. I mean he had been practically locked down in his life and what he done for so long and now he was free, but he was also falling in love. Richard's first gift to himself for his freedom was to buy himself a nice guitar, as he had given up playing years ago, so he saved for a few months and was able to get it just before Christmas. He started writing songs again, as he did back when he was in his teens. It was different this time though, he used to write about life and how cruel it was, but now all he could write about was love and hope. Well Richard truly felt that he had found love, and that all lives problems had happened in order for things to work out like this, for him to find Nicky. It was Nicky's first Christmas without her ex David, but she loved Christmas with her kids and visiting her family so she was too busy to think about it. Nicky had a job too working part time for the hospital as she was working towards qualifications in psychology and nursing.

From: Nicky> nicky@mynl.com
Sent: 26 December
To: Rich> richard@mynl.com
Hey what's up? ...well I just had my turkey dinner again too stuffed...its gross....it was very good though I am the queen of cooking turkeys...it was that tender this year that you could cut it with the side of a fork...was yummy anyways that's not my point here ....so ya we are getting a blizzard tonight and on the weather network it just keeps saying warning blizzard in big red letters...scary eh.....so I might end up with no power tonight I will still go on the usual time but if I disappear at some point in the night that's why...it hasn't started yet though...we are getting 45-60cm tonight and tomorrow..now that's a white Christmas

eh.....just typical weather for Cape Breton....they are closing the causeway too so it must be a good one....well I have to go for now and clean up this place try to find the rest of my kitchen and living room...so I hope to talk to ya soon, mwah infinity...I love you, see ya Nicky.

From: Rich> richard@mynl.com
Sent: 31 December
To: Nicky> nicky@mynl.com

Hey, sorry I haven't got back to you sooner. All that snow sounds crazy! We don't really get snow here in Ireland, like we get tiny bits in January some years but I don't think I can remember ever seeing snow on a Christmas day, so I think you're very lucky there... I've just put Ria to bed and well she has a bad cold, so she kept on waking herself up because she can't breathe through her nose cause it's all blocked. I had to go down the chemists and buy some stuff to put on her pillow so hopefully that helps and she will sleep through the night. I don't like seeing her unwell, like ya get this helpless feeling and yea I know she only has a bad cold but sure it's still not nice. Anyways I'll catch up with you soon xxx

From: Nicky> nicky@mynl.com
Sent: 31 December
To: Rich> richard@mynl.com

Well made it back in one piece weeeeeee.....I just got home about an hour ago I stayed at my friend Lisa's last night....I had an alright time....I was up dancing and singing on the stage... was too funny....apparently I just wouldn't stop dancing it was fun though.....God I wished that you were there....would have made the night complete eh....we definitely have to go out when I come over....I can't wait....so I hope you are doing a bit better tonight....I am glad to hear that Ria is doing better....it is hard for them when they are that young because they always breathe through their nose...my two used to have those suckie things too....it's hard on them eh....but still good that she is doing better....well have a great day today and I hope to talk to you real soon....mwah infinity, I love you Richard you amazing fella.....I talked about you last night quite a bit Lisa thinks it's cool and would like to meet ya but in good time eh....you would like her she is too funny....anyways I have to go and play with the kids.....I haven't slept yet but it's all good....I think the best moment of my night was walking in the door this morning and making them some breakfast....I missed them...ok I have to go....mwah, talk to you soon, I love you, Nicky.

Lisa was Nicky's closest female friend, they were really close, and great drinking buddies. One of the things about Nicky is that she appreciated the small things in life, like making breakfast, or sitting on her back porch watching a thunderstorm miles away and the lightening. She had this way about her that would make you look twice at things in life again. Some people can walk through life and never stop to appreciate some of life's perfect complexities. Now with Nicky in Richard's life he felt that everything was new and everything was fresh. Excited and hopeful about the New Year ahead, he spent New Year's celebrating with Ria. He only had the small box room at his parent's house then, so him and Ria slept topsy-turvy on the bed when she stayed at the weekends. He would love Ria waking him up at six in the morning and he'd take her downstairs so he could make her breakfast while she watched cartoons. They sent each other cards at Christmas, but as Richard opened his a letter fell out, inside the card it read the usual 'season's greetings and best wishes for a happy new year' and so he read the letter.

Dec 5th / 04
Richard
Well I figured I may as well write a little letter here to go with the card and all. Bare with me here, I don't think I have ever written a letter before, well other than a cover letter for a resume. I do hope that you have a great Christmas with lots of love and family and friends to

celebrate with, I hope this year you find the happiness that you truly deserving of. Richard, should I address you as Richard or Rich? Anyways, Richard, I like Richard, I have done nothing but smile ever since we first spoke. I feel so thankful and very much happy to have had the chance to have known you this far, and I hope to continue to stay in contact with you, as I feel myself liking you all the more every time we talk. You are amazing man; never forget that, because I know myself that even if we lose contact by some misfortune in the future I will always remember you, you're kind words and the ease at which you brought a smile to my face. So thanks for that, thank you for your friendship, a friendship which I believe may last a lifetime. I don't think for one second that the Atlantic Ocean will put a stop to this one. God there are just so many things I would like to say here, it's hard to bring to words eh. Well I look forward to meeting you in the New Year; I get excited whenever I think about going over there. I have always wanted to go there for as long as I can remember. And to meet someone as wonderful as you, will make it all the more worthwhile. This is strange isn't it, I honestly never thought that it was possible to feel the way I do for someone I have hardly known. What if?.... that is the constant question that comes to mind whenever I am just sitting here thinking of you, I don't know exactly what it is I am feeling at the moment, all I do know is I welcome it and will continue to enjoy it. So have a Merry Christmas and a very Happy New Year!!! Will speak with you soon, mwah infinity, hugs and kisses, Love, Nicky xo

Valentine
Chapter2

From: Nicky> nicky@mnl.com
Sent: 01 January
To: Rich> richard@mynl.com
Hey what's up? Well I love you...mwah....I am not sure what time
I will be on tonight...I am just leaving here in like ten minutes dad
invited me and the kids over for dinner and I don't know when I
will get back may be too late for you....but if I don't get on tonight
I will talk to you very soon I am working an evening shift though
tomorrow that's a 3.00 to 11.00pm shift so I won't be on tomorrow
night either sucks yes it does but I love you.....I hope you are
feeling better I enjoyed your company here last night and when I
went to bed I had the best sleep ever...must have been dreaming
about you, mwah....ok well I have to go I will talk to you soon,
have a great day tomorrow if I don't catch up with ya then....I will
miss you, mwah, sweet dreams, hugs kisses and love infinity
Nicky.
From: Rich> richard@mynl.com
Sent: 03 January
To: Nicky> nicky@mnl.com
Hi babe...
Don't know what happened last night...you went offline...then
my computer crashed on me....well anyways...hope you are ok
babe.... well I managed to get out today for a bit...though I had
slept in till two in the afternoon so by the time I got up and got
ready and all....well I went to the shops...got another book and
my pens and stuff ready for my course....then I went for a drive in
my car up the mountains and ended up at the Blessington lakes
where I pulled into one the car parks and went for walk around
some of the lake...as the sun was setting....was nice to get some
fresh air...and walk on sand...and see a bit of the countryside,

I'll send you some pictures later....then I headed home then for
Sunday dinner....well babe...I hope work was not too hectic for
ya....miss you....
Mwah infinity
Rich
From: Nicky> nicky@mnl.com
Sent: 03 January
To: Rich> richard@mynl.com
Hey what's up I am so sorry....I just came in the room and
you were flashing? there...I came in a while ago to check the
messages seen you left one I went to get cup of coffee and then
was going to send ya one back anyways I got side tracked when
I went out there so I missed ya sorry for that...God I have missed
you....the other night I went to put Gavin back to bed he was up
half the night wanting his dad it was strange because he hasn't
done that in a long while then when I got back I was signed out
again then I didn't have an Internet connection ......anyways I
figured it out it was because this laptop was new so it had to be
registered for the connection I wasn't aware that I had to do it
myself but I did it so now I am here......sorry though I did I miss
you and I am happy that you got yourself out for a while...and the
walk around the lake well I think it sounds beautiful there....so
you are all set now for your course?....I just found out today that
I am going back to class tomorrow...I thought I had another week
off..Lauren goes back tomorrow too so I am in for a busy day
here...I will be on tonight the usual time if you are on I would love
to catch up with ya then...right now I have to be going....I have so
much to do....I booked off work tonight and I am getting changed
back to two evening shifts a week and weekends...so it not too
bad....I can't believe I was off for a month and it's over already.....
mwah, mwah, mwah, mwah, mwah, mwah, mwah, mwah, mwah,
mwah, mwah, mwah, mwah........... + mwah infinity...we'll talk to
you soon I hope you have a great day....I love you...hugs and
kisses, Nicky.
From: Rich> richard@mynl.com

Sent: 17 January
To: Nicky> nicky@mynl.com
Wow that email...oh my God....some of them picks you sent
me of you were amazing, you're so sexy...so just sending ya
a little email to say I love ya lots and I just can't wait to be with
you....133 days to go till you're due to come over but I'm sure
that's probably bout half way from when if you think of when
we first had our first conversation...you know the one where
you asked me all about Ireland because you was coming over
here...? Well love is something special and some people never
experience it in their whole lives so I know I will treasure every
minute with you. mwah mwah infinity
p.s...In the chance that I might build a time machine I will flick
forward to the 30th of May ok? And in the even more unlikely
event of me winning the lotto.....you will find an Irishman at your
door the next day.........
p.s.s...Love you mwah mwah mwah
From: Nicky> nicky@mynl.com
Sent: 18 January
To: Rich> richard@mynl.com
Ok, ok well that's it.... I can't sleep here...guess I have a few
things on my mind I have tried to go to sleep honestly I have
but I can't seem to get comfortable at all I am freezing here I
think I got a chill when I was shovelling...what a mess it was half
solid ice...but I am still alive and very much in love with you so
why the hell am I complaining? I should just shut up and go to
sleep eh...well I will as soon as I tell you how much it means to
me to have finally found you...I believe in my heart you are the
one I have always been looking for and yes it does sound a bit
off base to say that but to me well not really....I was laying there
thinking about you ...thinking God wish you were now....I really
don't like to sleep alone...I never did....and wow I looked at those
pictures again of Ireland that you sent me and I love them all...I
so want to be there....soon enough...God it is hard to wait for
something eh.....I am just laying there my mind is racing and my

19

heart is too....I love you very much I seriously cannot wait to see you standing before me and I can finally say it....but after I do I tell ya well I am just going to have to kiss you and claim being in your arms as my favourite place in the world...would that be ok....well I will miss talking to you tomorrow but we will talk again on Wednesday...its only one day I know but you wow me and well one day is now a lot...strange eh...I never imagined this happening the way it did but I am very much happy that it did.... and yes I remember the first of our conversations....I believed I was wowed just as much then too just didn't realize it at the time...Richard I love you...it's now going on 2.00am I have to get up in say 4hrs weeeeeee...I wish that you were here to hold me all night while I sleep....really do need that right now....I am sorry. I should go....before I start to sound all needy and what not...but ya it would be nice....maybe that's what I can do eh I will imagine you are here with me just for tonight and fall asleep in your arms...that would be the best sleep ever I imagine...ok well talk to you soon have a great day today...I know I will because you are in my heart and Richard well I love you so much...so have a good one..... many kisses and hugs and all that jazz....infinity....mwah love ya, Nicky.

From: Rich> richard@mynl.com
Sent: 18 January
To: Nicky> nicky@mynl.com

Hey sexy, sorry that you have a chill eh, if I was there I'd give you a massage all over till you was feeling better. Though if I was there it would have been me out shovelling the snow, it's unreal for me to even think about what that is like cause I can't imagine what it would be like to be around so much snow. I have been thinking a lot about me and you and everything that's going on between us.   It's hard to put into words here but I will try my hardest for you cause I think it's important that you know how I feel about you. For starters I think you are so amazing, your smile, your personality and well just everything really to be honest. I have never felt so in love in all my life and you just

20

make me feel complete and I find that so more amazing because of how we met and the very slim chance that we ended up talking that night. There's nothing more in this life right at this moment that I would want more than to hold you in my arms, to make love to you through the night and express my love for you. I miss you more and more each day xxx love you xxx talk to you soon xxx
From: Nicky> nicky@mynl.com
Sent: 19 January
To: Rich> richard@mynl.com
Hey what's up? Thanks so much for all your messages I did love them all...just what I needed after my night...it was a wild one.... must be a full moon????? ...something was up tonight....not going there right now though ...trying to relaxing myself and my mind enough to chill out and get some sleep I am so very tired... Richard that message...wow I almost cried...not sad though it was great to hear what you think of all this and me and you...I do love you and well all I can say is you do wow me...I don't think in all my life have I ever known anyone that would say any of that.. so it does mean a lot I love to hear about what you are thinking and how you feel about things... anything you're thinking about... you are amazing on so many levels...and as tired as I am now after reading those well I feel happy so thanks for that...I really needed that..as you get to know me more you will find out that I do take a lot of things I see and do at work home with me and it is hard on the head at times and well I can't exactly mention everything that does go on there for many reasons...but that was well just perfect...so thanks...I do hold some stuff back but I wouldn't exactly say its secretive but I try not to let a lot bother me all that much ya know...it's like I will have like a tonne of things on my mind and well I just try and keep it to myself most of the time...as I said before I am saving it for the midlife crisis... someday I will just have the major meltdown I suppose but for now it's all good eh...God you just make me so happy I am smiling here it's amazing how you make me feel like this...I love it so bring it...and I love you very much Richard...I would type more

but I really have got to go to bed I am worn out and need a bed in a bad way here....I love you I love you I love you infinity...mwah, mwah, mwah infinity...hugs and kisses and lots and lots of love, talk to you soon, have a great day, miss ya love ya, Nicky.

From: Rich> richard@mynl.com
Sent: 22 January
To: Nicky> nicky@mynl.com

Hey babe, I am sorry here but I think I need to vent here a bit. I went to collect Ria today from her mum's house and well when I turned up at Ann's home there was another car and I guess it was the guy now that she is seeing and it was his car, and well it's not that that bothered me cause I don't care who she's with or anything but when I was walking past the car I noticed that Ria's car seat was in the back of his car and well I'm not very happy about it. I mean, who is this guy? What right does he have to be driving my daughter around; she's my daughter and not his. So ok I am a bit messed up here over this and I am sorry here for going on about it, I just wish I could be there for Ria more, you know what I mean? I am going to try and push it out of my mind here so I can enjoy the rest of the time that Ria is here. Maybe talk to you later if you are online?! Miss you lots xxx

From: Nicky> nicky@mynl.com
Sent: 22 January
To: Rich> richard@mynl.com

Hey what's up? well I just finished watching a movie...I don't know why I am sending you this...guess I was thinking about you... as I do...I hope you have a much better day today and have a great time with Ria...she does sound to me to be a wonderful little girl...and I know that you are a wonderful daddy well cause you are such an amazing person...and...well......I love you....I think that I will skip going to the spa with Lisa and just spend some time with my two tomorrow ...I think they need me more than they are able to express....you know I never mentioned it on the phone but when I picked up Lauren today I had to have a meeting with her teacher....it wasn't all bad though...Lauren is a smart little girl and sometimes maybe too smart eh....the teacher was concerned that at times it's like she dazes off like she is just not listening....I never realized it till now that maybe she did take me and David's' breaking up as hard as I had thought....I love her so much....I am actually in tears right now...so ya what's up??....so ya I think will find something to do with them tomorrow...try and make things I don't know better somehow.....I am sorry for putting this on you....I suck....I may not even send this to you anyways....and I know you said that you don't mind if I ever need to get something off my mind but...it's just the way I am it's how I deal with things I just try and forget...although sometimes like now I will be here alone and I start thinking things...Lauren is just me...when I look at her I see me....I was around her age when my parents split up....and to tell you the honest truth I don't know if I have ever been able to deal with that myself...so I see her as me.....oh this is too hard....I just hope that somehow she turns out to be better than me..able to handle things better...stronger.....oh wow this is too sad...enough of that I don't want to cry.....it's funny you know I have a puff with my sister Emma every now and then....and lately well I just do it to forget about a lot of things I have never dealt with in my life and when I am high it has it good points but most of the time like now....I come to these conclusions about things in my life...it's like I remember...anyways back to Lauren for a bit...see when I was her age I blamed myself for mom and dad splitting up...I was devastated...I would always try and get them back together but it never worked...I understand why that's now..but I at the time I felt it was cause of me....long story...so I am guessing that's the way she feels now..like it's her fault somehow....but like I said I just didn't realize it till now...and I know Gavin takes it hard too he gets up every night ..actually he should be up in another ten minutes or so...he gets up the same time every night looking for his dad....sometimes I don't even know if he is awake....oh Richard I am so sorry for this just in case I do send this ....I would love to tell you a lot about me that you don't know.....nothing bad though...just my issues right...like you have shared some of yours with me ....but I feel like if I do that....then I may be far too complicated to even be worth getting to know more about me...because really at times I don't know myself....but someday I will figure it all out.....and for now I am just going to try and be there more for the kids. They need me and I need them too.... and I think you really did have a bad day eh...I am sorry that you did and I am sure no matter whose car your daughter may ride around in she knows you are her daddy and I know you will always be there for her and she knows that too...so don't stress it....so just keep being there for her....and I tell ya she will never forget....you are an amazing bloke......and wow I love you..... well I think I have realized enough for one night and now I need to stop the tears here and get some rest...and thanks in case I do send this....if any of this even makes sense I do feel a little better...well again have a great day...I am sure you will enjoy every moment with her ok...and I can't wait to hear all about it. I will catch up with ya soon...I love you Richard and ya know what I think I will send it....why not eh...somehow I feel like well it's ok....there I shared one of my biggest issues that from time to time...really gets to me still...my parents divorce...but now that I think about it I was honest right from the start I told you that I had issues with the concept of marriage well cause I was a child of divorce...but now that I think about it...maybe I just think too much here eh...anyways I think maybe it's not so much the marriage part of it that I find so scary..but maybe it's my undealt with issues...which in turn make me perceive the whole concept of it as eventually ending up alone...ok ok now I am going too far with this here..anyways have a good one tomorrow....have a great day with Ria...and you mentioned again not being there for her as much as you would like well the that I say...being one that missed my dad a whole lot when I was younger....the time you do have with her make the very best of it that you can...because she will remember that....and she will know what an amazing daddy she has.....so again it doesn't matter what other men may come

into her life down the line....you will always be her number one....
so don't stress it....I love you ...mwah...mwah...mwah infinity...ok
got to get some sleep...be dreaming of you...as always....and I
am now smiling...so thanks again...and sorry again for saying all
this....talk to you soon...I love you, Nicky.
From: Rich> richard@mynl.com
Sent: 22 January
To: Nicky> nicky@mynl.com
Hey babe, listen thanks for the reassurance about the Ria stuff,
I really was freaking out over it. And well I enjoyed reading the
rest of your email, I'm glad you can share that kind of stuff with
me now, and well the more you tell me actually the more about
you I fall in love with, so yea keep it all coming cause I want to be
more in love with you each day. I know you have issues around
the marriage stuff and I do understand what you were saying
about it all, and hey listen we can take everything at what speed
you need to go at and that's ok with me. Love you lots xxx talk to
you soon xxx
From: Nicky> nicky@mynl.com
Sent: 23 January
To: Rich> richard@mynl.com
Hey what's up?...Well it's snowing again here...suppose to get
15cm this afternoon...then 30-35 tonight..blizzard eh...then
another 20-30 for the day tomorrow so looks like no school again
tomorrow weeeeeeee....only thing is is that every time I try and
sign into messenger it won't let me or I get signed out says the
service is temporarily unavailable....so I think it's the weather
causing it....so if I can't get on tonight I will call you if you don't
mind.....but I will still try and go on the same time as I usually
do...and hey thanks for calling me this morning that was cool....I
love you...it was strange though because in a way I kind of
knew it was you...I must have been dreaming about ya....when
I did eventually get up I thought you calling me was part of my
dream...then I checked the phone and I was like oh he did call
cool....mwah I love you Richard...ok I have to go and do a few

things here and I will be on later if it lets me if not I will call ya ok....mwah infinity...talk to you soon...hope you had a great day...I love you, Nicky.

Nicky sent Richard this link on a website. It was a weird website, kind of like made out that it's Irish but it wasn't really. You could send funny ecards off it and Richard and Nicky used to send them every now and again. What he loved most about this site was that you could click on a link that would show you road cameras from around the area where Nicky lived. Richard could never really believe her about all the snow until he seen it with his own eyes. He thought it was fantastic just seeing that snow fall so heavy and could flick between the cameras to see different places. Anyways it was the end of January and he felt like he needed to give Nicky some sort of commitment. Ria was up for the weekend and he took her into Dublin city centre with two hundred euro on him. They went up one the main streets in Dublin where there are a lot of travel agents. In the shopping centre near to where Richard lives, they just do trips like Spain and Greece kind of summer breaks but he wanted to go to Canada not Europe. So he walked into the first one he seen was advertising Canada on the posters on the wall. It was Saturday morning and it was empty, just two girls there working on duty, he took off Ria's heavy bright pink jacket and got the usual 'awwws' from the girls working there, well I mean Ria was just so cute with her blond curls. Anyways, he asked details for Nova Scotia and walked out with a booking reservation, Richard had paid the deposit on a trip to go over to see Nicky at the end of October. I don't know why he picked those dates, for some reason they just came into his head at the time. I guess he thought it would take him ages to save up the money to go over there. The flights were going to be 700 in total to fly as far as Halifax, there was a changeover in Heathrow. Halifax

26

was about a four hour drive to Sydney which is where Nicky lived. I guess he'd figure out the rest of the transport later, and was just happy to have it booked.

From: Rich> richard@mynl.com
Sent: 27 January
To: Nicky> nicky@mynl.com
Hello babe, well I sat down with my guitar today and came up with some nice tune but lacking some lyrics but hey it can be a work in process....but I do love writing songs...especially when they send a shiver down your spine when you get something good together. So I had my interview today on my lunch break... it went quite well and they will let me know by Tuesday next week whether I have been successful in my application...but it sounds like a nice company and I think it would be a good improvement for me. So like my bosses have not a clue to the fact that I am thinking of leaving......and yet another girl at work confronted the management today....it was one of their top people so it sent the showroom manager into a state of chaos.....and he ran around in a panic looking for Nicholas the branch manager. Well I'm not going to get revenge and leave them in shit ....I just think at this point it would be in my interest to move on.... besides why not ...I mean I know I can get more money elsewhere....money isn't that important to me but might come in handy for some spending money for when I am in Canada....or when I want to buy something nice for Ria for her birthday or whatever....I mean if I was a job I really liked I would put up with bad wages but I think at this stage I have more respect for myself than to do that for a company which simply does not appreciate the few good staff that it has....well anyways...mwah.
  I thought about you and me a lot today....sort of thinking down the line and stuff and it was all good...I know in myself that I have gone through a lot of changes in the last six months....learning who I am and who I want to be....and I know there are still things I am working on and things take time in that sense but maybe the fact that I don't meet you face to face till May is maybe a

good thing because I do have a few things I need to iron out in my head.....and although my heart is now in Canada.....exactly where I want it to be.....my mind is still working through a lot of stuff that I know is there.....and well I have come a long way and I'm so proud of myself for being able to work through all this and I know that meeting you now at this point has some sort of plan in the big picture.....despite it being hard to feel this way about you when you are so far away....I look the future with a big smile on face. I want to answer something for you too.....do ya know when I say "God owes me one"....well back in the summer when I was on my disappearing act to London.....one day I was having it really tough and I sat in the middle of a park...in the middle of the field....and basically had a big argument with God about everything I have faced in my life and how I had not been happy in years.....and well do ya remember in like *Forest Gump* when he is out in the prawn trawler boat fishing and there is that big storm and his army friend have this big argument with God... well it was sort of like that....well anyway the point is...that after that I felt inside that somehow God will bring about a change in my life where I can be happy in myself and be around people who love me for who I am and that I would have some good times to make up for all the bad....so anyways.....bring it eh
Love you loads
xxxxxxxxxxxxxxxxxxxx
Rich
From: Nicky> nicky@mynl.com
Sent: 28 January
To: Rich> richard@mynl.com
Hey what's up?...well boy ya know how much I love you eh...and if ya don't I promise I will show ya just how much very soon and I also promise to show you for a very very long time if you will let me....I hope that everything works out for you in regards to your new work endeavours....and hey to me it doesn't matter what you do your still amazing....and I can't wait to hear your music....I bet it just wonderful...you are very talented...just amazing...

but you know that eh...and I can't wait to meet you in person...
it will be like finally....finally I can tell you that I love you...finally
I can see you can kiss you...can be with you...wow just thinking
about it makes me the happiest girl alive here....you do that..
You make me happy...when I talk with you... every time... I just
think to myself why did you take so long to come into my life....
just wowed...I love you...I really love you Richard....and hey I
mean that...and I also mean I love you just as you are.....so even
though you talk about things you have to deal with...and believe
me...I understand... I think you should be happy for yourself and
who you are now...everything has a way of falling into place...and
whatever is on your mind you know I am here for you...anything
at all...I am here....wishing I could be there but you get me...
soon enough eh?...and is that what you meant by that?....well
I know now that you are the one for me...I have never been so
sure of anything...and I also believe that when we meet it's going
to make it all the more true...so I think you may be right...and
bring it...well consider it brought....and then some....you make me
feel some unbelievable things...things I don't believe I have ever
experienced in my whole life...and it all feels so right...so good...
so amazing...but that's you...amazing you are...so thanks again
for making me the happiest girl alive I swear it....and I love you...
so I hope you have a great day today...I am going to go get some
rest here myself.....talk to you soon...mwah mwah mwah mwah
mwah mwah mwah mwah mwah infinity...I do love you so much
Richard....lots of hugs and kisses, Nicky.
From: Rich> richard@mynl.com
Sent: 2 February
To: Nicky> nicky@mynl.com
Well hi Nicky.....how are you? I miss you....well what a strange
day I have had, where do I start? Well let me see ....it was like
11 this morning and the boss called me in out of the blue and
said he was upping my wages by ten percent.....so I told him
I had been offered a job elsewhere and had really come in to
hand in my weeks' notice...and I explained all the problems and

difficulties I have been having and bout the other managers forcing me into working on the weekends when I can't because I have Ria.....well let's just say he wasn't happy with what he was hearing so he went and sorted most of it out in the hope I would stay. Well he has increased my wages to more than the other company offered me and promised to get everything else sorted out for me.....I mean Liam is the man at the top of the branch but he rarely deals with staffing problems anymore but I'm glad he went and sorted out things for me.....because I do like the job itself it's just all these other things that were being thrown at me... so I've decided to stay and put my trust in him to get it all sorted out for me where the other managers have let me down.... so anyways....what's up sexy...I love you mwah.

So like I got home and had my dinner and a shower. I headed down to the local shops to buy my lotto numbers for tonight and well popped into the chemist as well to try and get some more cream for the eczema...well she took one look at my arm and sent me off to the doctors.....so off went to the doctors....just in time before they were closing. So the doctor had a look and prescribed me some cream and gave me a repeat prescription. He also said that it was more than likely the shower gel that done it to me and that because I suffer from eczema I should not use shower gels because it will dry up my skin and agitate it.... well anyways glad to be getting it sorted out despite paying like 50 quid to see the doctor then another 15 quid for the cream... the robbers.. but like I knew what cream would work it's just that it needs to be on prescription which makes no sense at all.... ahhhhhhhhhhhh so here I am sitting on their edge of my bed in just my boxers waiting for this cream to soak in a little...lol..... though I do wish you were here to rub it into my back.....I can't exactly reach well Nicky I hope you have a nice day today and tomorrow and I will speak to you tomorrow normal time yeah? Love you loads.....mwah infinity
Rich
From: Nicky> nicky@mynl.com

Sent: 03 February 2005
To: Rich> richard@mynl.com
Well hey what's up? I miss you very much....but I have been
thinking of you all day so it's all good...my thoughts of you keep
me a very happy girl...well that's good news then eh about your
job....wow... well it's about time they did something there for you
eh...see you must be amazing even with your work...but hey
that's you... amazing...hey as long as you are happy that's all that
matters...I am happy for you either way...I love you Richard...my
day was very busy...I am just here now trying to get this paper
done before the sun comes up...weeeeeeeee...it's almost done
though I did some at work cause the census was low not much
to do there anyways today....it was a good day though ..can't
believe how much I really missed it...school was great...I went
to a meeting with the other honours students and the faculty in
regards to my thesis and seminar for next year....just going over
some available topics for research....I haven't decided what I
want to do yet...but I have till the summer to figure it out so it's
all good....this one is very important though so I don't think I will
put it off too much...this will be the deciding one for grad school...
other than that my day was great. Lauren went to skating today
at school....of course I forgot her skates so I went to the school
there at lunch and dropped them off to her I felt so bad about
forgetting but she made it in time...God I missed them today
too...I seen Gavin when I woke up for all of a half hour...while
rushing around.... and I won't see him till tomorrow afternoon
now...well hey that's good that you found out what caused your
skin to get irritated...so that's what they think it was the gel eh...
hopefully what the doctor prescribed will work out for you...it must
be bothering ya eh and yes if I was there I would put the cream
on your back...but then I would have to kiss you all better..and
well among other things eh....mwah I love you...........ok I just
have to say this here........you know I truly believe you are by far
the most amazing fella I have ever known...I do believe you when
you say you love me...before when it was said in the past well I

didn't trust it....but with you I trust it...and wow I really love you....
and am giving you my heart...I trust you with it....with no fear...
it is the best feeling I have ever known...so thanks....I know that
when I meet you it will be the best day...probably a day I have
waited for a very long time....cause I believe in fate and I feel you
Richard are the one I am meant to be waiting for and I really do
feel nothing but good things that will be..somehow...everything
feels so right not to be...you wow me x infinity...so I am here
waiting ever so patiently for the day I am finally in your arms...
soon to be my favourite place in the world...sometimes I will just
be sitting here and I think of meeting you...I think about kissing
you for the first time...and wow my heart just races like crazy...I
think about being able to well finally being able to tell you in
person that I do love you...I think about so much stuff..wonderful
stuff and I smile....like right now just smiling....I love you.......
alright well I should be getting back to my paper...so I will talk to
you tomorrow ..I hope you have a wonderful day...and again I am
very happy for you...amazing you are....well I have to say it again
here just because eh....Richard I love you...mwah infinity,
Nicky

Richard and Nicky sent each other some stuff for Valentine's
Day. Richard sent a nice card over to Nicky and also arranged
some romantic e-cards which she enjoyed. Nicky sent to
Richard also a nice card and some pictures of her and her
family and also she sent him another letter just as she had at
Christmas which was a nice surprise for him as he had not
expected anything. The letter read as follows...

Jan 14th
Richard
Hey what's up? Well I was just sitting here thinking
about you and your amazingness eh, so I figured I
would write you a letter. I took the day off school today,
just really tired today and I have some things to do
this afternoon...no worries though I am not missing a

whole lot today. So it's all good. God, really don't like writing on lined paper as it ends up being too small, but hey it's all I could find. I loved talking to you on the phone last night...amazing voice...wow I just love you so much. Every day I look forward to talking to you... Its definitely the best part of my day...and honestly, I would never have thought it would have been possible to fall in love...so fast...so much...for someone I have never met...must be meant to be I suppose...I am glad I found you...I love you..and every time we chat I fall more and more in love with you...it will be a dream come true for sure...mwah infinity...I wish for so many things...but I understand that if it is to be it will be and so I have decided just let it be eh...but I am enjoying this far... so bring it...I am ready for it...I have fallen for you... you are a part of my life...I feel a part that was always waiting for me..I believe you are the one I am meant to be with...and so I will wait for you be patient and I am still smiling here...I am a very happy girl...and it's all because of you...Richard wow I do really love you!!! O.K so another reason I am writing this to you is because I thought as you have done for me, it would be nice to send it with something to have got for you......it's not much...but I hope you like it...mwah, mwah, mwah. You know, I have always wanted to go to Ireland for as long as I can remember. As a child I remember my granddad telling me about his dad and where he was from...what he was like...I also remember just now sitting on his knee...he would always be play that traditional music...I loved it...I miss him...he was a wonderful man...ok enough of that though...I don't want to be sad..I want to remain happy...anticipate my trip over to see the things he...well my dad have talked about...and now of course to meet you...I love you... Well I should try and wrap this up here I have to go pick up Lauren soon from school and Gavin is looking for his lunch. I could just keep writing here...it comes easy...I feel like with you it doesn't matter what I talk about...I just have so much to say...I just hope I have not bored you to tears reading it, as I do have a tendency to ramble on...so sorry for that...k well I hope your having a great day, and I hope your little one is doing well...really can't wait to meet you both...alright, talk to you soon, mwah infinity as always, I wish you nothing but the best, I love you very much, Nicky xo xox o

Something Blue And I Miss You
Chapter3

From: Rich> richard@mynl.com
Sent: 15 February
To: Nicky> nicky@mynl.com
Well I'm missing you.....I hope you had a good day today....I
was quite busy at work today and got through a good bit of
study when I got home....I actually got the first draft to the first
half of my assignment done...so well pleased with myself well
I can't wait to see you tomorrow night and well I was going to
ask ya something ....did you say you were or weren't working
on Saturday? Hey listen I hope tomorrow brings you nice
weather.....some nice dreams and some smiles....and well I will
be on here waiting for you at the end of the day...I love you loads
and loads and loads
xxxxxxxxxxxxxxxxx
Rich
P.S. did u wear blue today?
mwah
From: Nicky> nicky@mynl.com
Sent: 16 February
To: Rich> richard@mynl.com
Hey I miss you so much too...mwah infinity...good to hear you
are doing ok with your course ...and yes blue ...you're too good
at guessing eh...so I suppose I owe you another...it's all good
...and no I am not working Saturday, I do have to work tomorrow
or maybe I should say today from 7am-7pm...same shift for
Thursday and Friday will be a backshift 7pm-7am...but I will
speak to you tomorrow night and I can't wait...really missed you
today...work was ok?...not good not bad...Richard I love you...I
have to go get some sleep...I really wish you could be here with
me right now... to be able to cuddle up to you in bed and kiss

you...just to be in your arms now would be in heaven...well I hope you have a great day...I really would say so much more but I have to go back into work in five hours...but I will be dreaming of you here lying next to me...Oh I wish for that so much...soon.... mwah mwah mwah...I love you, Nicky.

When Richard had asked if Nicky was wearing blue, he was asking about what underwear she had on. You see they had this little game they would play when they were chatting on messenger and on their web cameras. Basically Richard would get a guess and only got one guess, but if he got it right then Nicky would strip down and show him what he had guessed correctly. It was their way of throwing in a bit of sexual excitement when they were not able to be there with each other in the same room. It did help that Richard was a very good guesser, and he would in turn strip for Nicky sometimes too.

The next night they met up on messenger at the usual time. They get past the pleasantries and talk about the day that they had. So Richard guesses again about what she is wearing. He guesses that she is wearing purple and besides even if he got it wrong, she still owed him from last time. He sees Nicky nod her head to her web camera, and then stand up. Nicky is a very beautiful woman, about 5'10 in height and a size 10 waist and has some very nice curves. She teasingly unzips her top, slowly revealing her blue lace bra underneath. Removing her top she leans forward showing off her cleavage in front of the screen. Richard's heart starts to race as Nicky turns, and undoes her jeans button and zip and leans over pulling her jeans down, showing off her blue lace hot pants. She checks back on the screen to see Richards face and see's that he's really enjoying it. She loved to tease, and so did he. He removes his top displaying his quite muscular arms and shoulders. Richard had a rugby type build, which is what Nicky loved. Richard loved how sexy Nicky was, it seemed to him that she had the perfect body, she wasn't skinny, not fat, she was just right in-between, with really curvy hips and she had naturally large breasts. The way that they could both strip off showed not only how comfortable they were with each other, as to strip on camera over the internet involves a lot of trust so that you don't end up on some porn site.

From: Nicky> nicky@mynl.com
Sent: 20 February
To: Rich> richard@mynl.com
Hey what's up?...I hope you had a wonderful weekend...mine was alright...I went out and played pool last night with Thomas...I was super tired though so I ended up getting in a like 10.00pm....then I just crashed...I tell ya though it was by far the best sleep I had had in a long time...I think I might get out of here for a little while today...just go for a walk or something it's so sunny out... but it's also so cold today...not sure what I want to do yet...but I miss you and can't wait to talk to ya later...oh Richard...I just think about you all the time and its really all good eh...meeting you is going to be a dream come true...I am getting more and more excited each day here...I love you so much...well I have to go for now...going to go and jump in the shower...but I will be thinking about you so mwah infinity, talk to you soon, hugs , kisses, I love you, Nicky.
From: Rich> richard@mynl.com
Sent: 20 February
To: Nicky> nicky@mynl.com
Hey babe, I'm glad you had a good night out last night with your cousin. Hey would you like some company for the shower, let me scrub your back? Or maybe just kiss you all over eh....I wish.... hey but soon enough though we could do that, and maybe sometime we could go for a game of pool too, though I'm not that good at it, and I'm sure you'll beat me but it's all good. I'm not long out of bed here myself, I think I am just going to have a lazy day here or something, or maybe I'll go over to the shops

for a bit?! Anyways, do you fancy meeting up online later for a few drinks and nice long chat? Love you xxx Rich.

From: Nicky> nicky@mynl.com
Sent: 22 February
To: Rich> richard@mynl.com

So yea, I love you....I really wanted to talk more with you tonight but Thomas wanted someone to talk with and well smoke a joint with....and you know what.... I think I don't want to do it anymore...so that's that I am not going to do it anymore....I don't need to anymore...I mean I only do it for well reasons but I mean I am happy...you make me so happy and it's so real you know.... so I don't need the false happy high anymore....God it's late I am finally coming down off it....that was like almost four hours it was totally bizarre....I was actually scared...another reason why I am not doing it anymore....anyways I am just rambling on and on here...Richard do you know how much you make me happy... how much I love you?....all I have to do is just to think of you and my heart goes crazy here...wowed for sure....in awe...amazed...I love you....I really do love that song...I am listening to it now... before I go to bed...wish you were here...God I just need you so bad....I feel like I should be so thankful to have found you....I just know you are the one..I know because it is like nothing before...I want to be with you...I have never felt so sure about anything before...you are amazing....and I really do believe in fate....I love you....and I give you my heart...it's really all good...well I should go to bed here I have a long day tomorrow eh...I do wish that you could be here...I want to be in your arms...to feel you next to me...kissing me and me kissing you right back...loving you forever...mwah infinity have a great day...talk to you soon, I love you, Nicky.

From: Rich> richard@mynl.com
Sent: 23 February
To: Nicky> nicky@mynl.com

Hi Nicky...my queen

So like I've just come online now...I was watching *Terminator*

3....I had never seen it before....it was cool... so like thanks for your email...it's hard for me to reply to it because it seems a lot of the stuff I am feeling in my heart is the same as you feel for me ... and well I don't want to say it back in the same way so that it will sound like I am just copying what you say. Well I do want to say that I love you loads and loads....and it's not face value love and it's not as they say "in lust"....I just know and feel deep down in my heart a real warm love for you that makes me feel happy from the inside out. In any relationship I have had in my entire life I have not felt this way...maybe in the past I talked myself into certain situations... and made myself become someone that provides every need for my girl and ignored all my own needs so that inside I was always unhappy. Things are so different in my head right now....I learnt back in August how to take a step back and evaluate myself to see what's going on in my head. When I do that now...let me tell you what I see...I see that my heart is free from the hurt other people and myself has done to me over the years....I see that I now believe in life and that I can make a good life for myself...my daughter and hopefully you and your kids (plus 13 haha)...I hold a lot of hope in my heart that I have never experienced before. And well when I examine how things are in my head in reference to you...that's where I really surprise myself because boundaries that I have never felt comfortable breaking for any girlfriend before have just like opened like flood gates...things I thought I would never be comfortable with...I now am with you...

I guess what I am getting to that I know that me and you could really work....we can make it work...but when I say "make", I don't mean us putting up with each other unhappily because I really feel that we will make each other very happy for a long time...I love you for who you were, I love you for whom you are and I love you for who you will be.....just remember that it will be the two of us and only the two of us that will define our relationship....Different people in my life through the years told me that I am a guy who looks at things from a different way....

39

my mind is re-teaching itself like a computer almost....the family
I grew up in....the cultural and religious ways that were taught
to me are all being questioned in my head...not in a way of me
losing my identity of who I am but I think I am questioning the
beliefs of what was taught to me and asking are they true....
ok before I go off on even more of a tangent here I'll go back to
what I was trying to say is that....me and you....our relationship....
I would like us to open our minds rather than take the form of a
relationship which society tells us it should be....I will dedicate my
heart, my time , my love, my faithfulness and everything else like
my guitar playing and put it on OUR table and you can bring all
your stuff and put it on OUR table and I'm sure two smart people
like us can assemble something where we will both be very
happy....because it will be a relationship made to suit us and not
what society has told us to do ok I hope I am not sounding like a
head case here and I hope you understand what I'm saying....so
I'll stop here till I know eh? Well I missed you loads today, love
you mwah infinity
Rich
From: Nicky> nicky@mynl.com
Sent: 23 February
To: Rich> richard@mynl.com
I love you infinity...I am yours infinity and yes I understand you
completely...and I want to be with you so much...and I believe
that it is so right...I am so sure of us...and I am very happy at
this minute ...just lost for words...
....
....
.....ok enough dots...wow...you know I feel like I need someone
to pinch me here...Richard I love you...and I want everything
you want... I want it with you....you are the one...how I feel
for you is so intense....and it doesn't change it just gets more
and more intense...I believe we are meant to be and I know
in my heart we are...sometimes I will sit and think to myself is
it possible...me and you...in my heart I know it is and that's all

that matters anymore...and I do talk about you so much...I am always thinking of you...some people will be like well how do you know everything will work out between the two of you... you can't wait for something that might not work out...they say I am just a dreamer...but I don't agree with them at all... it makes perfect sense to me...I am in love with the most amazing man I have ever known...you Richard...you are the one...the way I feel is how I know it will be...it's far too real...too intense not to be...so yes I am up for just going with how we feel for each other and letting that be what guides us...wow I love you....I want to have a life with you and with our kids...and our future kids... I believe that all of that will be...and time is just an obstacle...but nothing more than that....so what....we have to wait...I would wait a lifetime just to be with you in the next one eh....soon...I will be with you soon...that's what I dream of at night..what I wish for when I am thinking of you...happiest girl alive....ok I have a secret I want to share with you...every night before I go to sleep....well you know that picture you sent me of you and Ria....well I never shut this laptop off I just leave it on all night....but I will put that picture up and go to bed and I lay there and I can see you...I pray for our future together...my sister says I am just so pathetic eh...but nope I am in love....in love with you Richard...heart and soul...ok well I have to go and read some stuff now....thanks for your message it makes perfect sense to me....and I feel the same way....and hey you're free to continue whatever you want to tell me....I understand I am feeling it too...and it is just wow so wonderful eh....so don't stop....I love you so much Richard, talk to you soon, mwah infinity, Nicky.
From: Rich> richard@mynl.com
Sent: 24 February
To: Nicky> nicky@mynl.com
I love you
It has been well over a year now since I first got my computer online, last Christmas I bought a ticket for Ann and Ria to head off to England to see Ann's relatives....hey it was a nice gift but I

did not want to go...I think it was around that point that I realised that I did not love Ann anymore....and well I then became immersed in being online...meeting new people...experimenting with cyber (I was a slut eh) but I knew in my heart I was not happy back then and well I had very little hope for the future I never mentioned why I had not been to my thinking place in that park for such a long time, the one that I went to the other week for a walk....well it was because the last time I was there....I sat there and had decided to give myself three months to sort myself out or I would just give up and kill myself.....though that was well before me and Ann split up....I guess I got there in the end and sorted myself out.....though it took more like year's than 3 months. Despite it being last June when me and Ann split I knew from Christmas that no love existed between her and me....and well I guess that's where Rachel slipped into my life....me and her met in a chat room.....but what grew over the following months was a good strong friendship .....I was not happy with Ann and Rachel was not happy with her husband... and she split from him months before I split with Ann....I know at the point of breakdown in my life, it was only a phone call from her that gave me an escape route to get myself sorted. So Ann and I split and I was asked to leave the house on Ria's birthday last year....a week later I walked onto the ferry to England and disappeared to England.....that was a freaky time in my life.....I don't think I slept at all very much....and every night was a total drinking session.....I was in a mess and so was Rachel and all her friends.....but somewhere in the madness.....and somewhere in the excessive amount of alcohol ....I changed inside....I had not lost any of my hatred for life but my want to kill myself drifted away. I was there just over five weeks and in my last week there I got talking to a girl in Ireland online and well she was instrumental in helping me through what happened as I returned home....God that was such a thing for me to come home! I think it felt nice to have someone on my side because at that stage I felt there was no one... a bit of romance developed and lasted a couple of months but it definitively was not meant to be and we went our separate ways at the end of August....but back when I was in England...I knew I would meet someone....and that she would make me happy...and that certain things would take place and that's how I would know that she would be the one for me. I had not thought about this again till last week when I realised that my need to talk to loads of people online and to search through chat rooms and the need to spend endless hours looking at this computer screen in the hope of finding what I was looking for.....it well had all disappeared without me realising that I had stopped....it was so strange to find that something I had become addicted to just disappear.....it is like you waking up one day and realising you had not had a smoke for 3 or 4 months and not even realised it!!! Well what I am getting at here is that went I look back to what I believed the right person would be for me and how they would take a hold of me I knew that went it happened that all the cyber....all the searching would stop....and that inside I would finally feel loved for who I am and that that woman would be the right one for me.....well Nicky I believe deep down in my heart that it is you....and even though we have obstacles to overcome...I believe that we can do it....and that love will conquer...mwah mwah mwah mwah

I love you, Rich

From: Nicky> nicky@mynl.com
Sent: 25 February
To: Rich> richard@mynl.com

Well, see there you go again making me all tearful here....I am not sad though....very much happy ...Richard I really love you too and I know this for sure...I want to show you my love for you... wishing you were here now...thanks for calling me I needed to hear you....I want to be in your arms ... to feel you next to me... to just love you completely and totally ya know....I find that as time gets closer to me coming over to see you...its more and more hard to be patient.....oh Richard, I truly believe you are the most amazing fella....I just know you are the one...I am so in love

with you...you are always in my thoughts....which I have to say
have been changing since we first started speaking....I mean
in the beginning I thought to myself that you were too good to
be real...but at the same time even at the start I never doubted
you for a second....I just believe in you....more and more as time
goes by....I think you are wow so amazing....so wonderful in so
many ways...just perfect....and I love you beyond words....never
felt this way in all my life....I love that you are you...that you are
honest with me about how you feel...I trust in you and I believe
in us....Richard you are so real...the way you make me feel is....
well if you don't know by now then just wait and see eh....I live
for the day to show you my love for you...and I know that day is
coming very soon....and I know that when I am over to see you
it's going to take a lot longer than just that trip...what I feel for
you is something I pray I will be able to show you for all my days
here on this earth...I love you so much....mwah mwah mwah
mwah infinity....those kisses and many more will be real soon...
makes my heart race when I think about that....very soon...it's
like each time we speak I fall more and more in love with you...
if that is possible....because this is so intense eh...it doesn't even
matter what we talk about..or if sometimes we don't have a lot
to say...it's just being able to hear your voice...or to see you...I
am happy...so very happy....you make me feel comfortable with
telling you anything....sometimes I wonder if I knew you before...
by some crazy chance at another time....because it's like the
most intense feelings I have for you...and I was a bit scared of
this at first, I have to admit it.....I was like wow wow wow wow
wow wow infinity what's up with this eh...but now I am sure in my
heart this is real....and I am truly wowed here for sure.....mwah...
another thing I had feared was that I was fallen in love with you
so fast so easy....but maybe there is no such thing as too fast
or too easy when it comes to true love...I think when something
like what we have here feels this real...this right....that it must be
meant to be eh...I am done questioning what I feel for you like I
did before....there is no need to...I mean I know how I feel and

I know how you feel and that's all that matters anymore...I love you Richard I love you so much....well I am going to go and read a little then watch something on TV....I feel so much more relaxed now that I am sending this to you.. I mean if you were here with me now I would have said it all to you...look in your eyes...kiss you and just spill it eh....God I wish you were here now or me there right now ...just to finally be together....very soon...well I hope you have a great weekend...I love you so much Richard....I love your name....I love everything about you and most of all I love that you are you...just you...and that's amazing for sure.... you're real and you are amazing....I'll be thinking about you... mwah infinity...I love you....I am yours infinity...I truly believe that...just as I know and trust and believe that you are the one I am meant to be with.....talk to you soon, I love you, Nicky.
From: Rich> richard@mynl.com
Sent: 02 March
To: Nicky> nicky@mynl.com
I missed you like crazy today...hope you are ok...mwah I love you
Rich
xxxxxxxx
From: Nicky> nicky@mynl.com
Sent: 02 March
To: Rich> richard@mynl.com
Hey what's up? I missed you like crazy too Richard...been thinking about you all day....I am just getting in now and checking the emails and that....but I will be on tonight ...I can't wait to talk with you later...I had such a busy last couple of days ....I just want to relax tonight....I am not going to do anything tonight....just want to talk with you....I love you so much..And yes I was happy yesterday....smiling at the thought of being with you soon.... so I will talk to you in a bit...I have to go do the supper thing. I am thinking something quick and easy...most likely I will order a pizza....yummy...I am starving I haven't had a decent thing to eat in the last couple of days eh....well mwah infinity...I love you, Nicky.

From: Rich> richard@mynl.com
Sent: 02 March
To: Nicky> nicky@mynl.com
Hey babe, I love you xxx. Well I'm looking forward to meeting with ya later, will be good for sure, and it's nice that you have been thinking about me, and well I have been thinking about you lots that's for sure. Hey what toppings do you like on a pizza? My favourite is ham and pineapple but all pizza is good in my eyes, did you ever try dipping it in salad cream, makes it ten times better! Anyways I'll see you later babe xxx miss you xxx.

From: Nicky> nicky@mynl.com
Sent: 06 March
To: Rich> richard@mynl.com
Hey what's up?....well I just got home....by far the worst night of my entire life eh.....I wish you were here....I could really go for a big hug right now....I love you so much....I should have stayed home.....I am so tired now....awful night....never going with Thomas again.....I didn't get high though even though there was plenty of opportunity for it...I felt like I was in a crack house..... what a dump....and the people there were just like yuck....I mean seriously if I ever reach that point in my life....kill me right on the spot.....horrible...just horrible....anyways I knew Thomas was a mess but I now know how much of a mess he is.....and wow...I am so angry about it....my God....I wish I could talk with you right now....maybe I should just go to bed and hope that everything I witnessed tonight was a real bad dream....I love you Richard.... wow I love you...I need you very much...and I understand that we have to wait some more....I will wait for you....I love you...no matter what....well I need a bed now....wish I could share mine with you....you are the one....I love you so much, Nicky.

From: Rich> richard@mynl.com
Sent: 18 March
To: Nicky> nicky@mynl.com
Well here I am sitting at home.....I just got out of the shower.... trying to get ready to go out.....I wish you were coming with

me....I love you so much and all I've done today is talk about you to people at work.....I really enjoyed last night especially when you stripped for me again, it was amazing, you are amazing...and I hope you did too...I love you I miss you I want to kiss you I want to show you how much I care for you xxxxxxxxxxxxxxxxxxxxxxxxxx xxxxxxxxxxxxxxxx

mwah infinity

I love you with all my heart

Rich

From: Nicky> nicky@mynl.com

Sent: 18 March

To: Rich> richard@mynl.com

Hey what's up? well I'm glad you enjoyed last night...I miss you I forgot to send you an email before I left....sorry about that I am just at Lisa's right now...having a couple of drinks and watching a movie....we aren't going out tonight we are just going to stay in tonight...tomorrow night though she wants to go to the bars.....I think I will stay here for the night ...but I should be back sometime tomorrow...if I don't get online tomorrow night I will give you a call before I go out...if that's ok with you? I will get back to ya either way...I love you so much....mwah infinity...talk to you soon...again I hope your night was great....I miss you...she thinks I am right nuts here sending you this email from her house...I just miss you is all and I love you very much...sweet dreams ..I will be thinking about you as I do....mwah... where do you want that eh...well wherever it is I will kiss you there infinity ...ok mwah talk to you soon...I love you, Nicky

From: Rich> richard@mynl.com

Sent: 20 March

To: Nicky> nicky@mynl.com

Hi babe...I hope you had a good night out....I tried buzzing ya earlier but must have missed ya unless you were still in bed...lol. Well I've been doing loads of study seeing as though I never got around to it last night....I'm about to head out for a while to get some fresh air.....so I hope you might be on later...I miss you....

Rich
From: Nicky> nicky@mynl.com
Sent: 24 March
To: Rich> richard@mynl.com
Hey what's up? ....alright well I went to sleep... I did...but now I just can't...I woke up and now I just can't sleep......oh I love you so much...and I promise to show you how I feel very soon.... Richard you are the one...and I love you....alright I'm going back to bed now....just had to tell you that I love you so much.... and I hope to hear from you soon...I hope you're having a great weekend with Ria....God I have missed you so much...I love you Richard...I love you I love you I love you....I don't know if you will be on tonight or if you will get this at all today...but if you do...I would love to call you just to hear your voice or you could call me....Richard I have thought about you a lot this weekend....I had an alright time I suppose but still something was missing...you...I miss you...well have a good one eh...talk to you soon...mwah infinity...I love you so much, Nicky.

Did I try my best?
Chapter 4

It was a Friday night again and Nicky had made some plans to go out partying. Sometimes Richard wouldn't hear from her much over the weekends, especially recently but they would always try and sneak in a quick chat on the phone or on messenger before they headed off on their busy social lives. Nicky had started her night out around at her aunty Julia's house, she met her cousin Thomas there and they sat there having a joke and a laugh with a few beers and they lit up a joint and passed it around and by this point they were getting into the 'Friday feeling'. Thomas's mate Jacob had come around, he was a tall guy, and wasn't properly shaved and was sporting a rough look and was wearing a camouflage army jacket in multiple green colours. Thomas's girlfriend Sophia also arrived, she was a lot different to Nicky, she was short and blonde and very petite, however and the party atmosphere was gathering momentum now that there were a few people there. The four of them shared another joint and a few more beers and then said their goodnights to Julia and headed off towards the local pool hall. The local pool hall was like a basement type place with just six tables and a bar, not lit up greatly, but used by many locals just as a starting point for their night out. Thomas sparked up another joint on the way down to the pool hall and they were all enjoying it and having a laugh. Sometimes being able to escape from the normal routine on Fridays is what makes people go so crazy on a night out. Nicky was no stranger to this, her Fridays usually went along the routine of David picking the kids up from her house (probably with some small altercation involved too) and then she'd pop on the chill out songs whilst she got ready to go out and meet her friends.

Thomas and Nicky had obviously been to this place many times and were not strangers to making bets and playing against other people that they would meet. It was that kind of place, a person secured the use of a table by putting down money on it, but they could just as easily say "play the winner?" for a match. It's a way of meeting new people and socialising and who knows maybe getting invited to parties or anything else that might be going on. There wasn't always money down on games to win though it would happen on the odd occasion. And so on this night Thomas and Nicky were having a game, well Nicky was having a game more like and Thomas was watching on, wishing he was that good! Two guys came up and put money down on the edge of the table asking to play the winner. Thomas went up to the bar to get a jug of beer, it was cheaper to buy the beer this way, and it meant one wasn't going to and from the bar all the time as the jug would last a while. The two guys introduced themselves to everyone, first there was Matt who was a reasonably tall broad shouldered guy in his twenties, he wore a backwards facing baseball cap, had a fair amount of stubble on his face and was reasonably good looking. The other guy Josh was a bit shorter than Matt and his hair style was outward pointing blond hair (with brown roots) and looked a bit more physically fit than his friend. They were both there with a couple of other friends or at least there were other people there who knew them.

The night continued, everyone was gone from being at the merry stage of drinking to the point where the room was starting to rotate a little. It was then that Thomas started to notice something dodgy about these two guys, they weren't in themselves weird or what they were doing wasn't weird but he just had a bad feeling about it. You see they were both blatantly paying lots of attention to Nicky and ok yes she's very good looking and does get attention, but she seemed drunker than everyone else.

"I don't like these guys" he whispered to Sophia.

"Ok, well what can we do eh?" she said.

"We could head to Herman's and hope they stay here" he said still whispering.

"Come on ......let's go" Thomas said in a commanding voice without mentioning where so that the two guys wouldn't know so that they could not follow. The last game of pool was finished anyways so they start getting their jackets on, and Sophia goes to the bathroom before they leave.

"Hey you want to stay with us?" Matt says to Nicky.

"Yea, we are heading off to a house party" Josh said.

"Hey that sounds good, I like parties" Nicky said.

"Well we're heading off to the clubs" Thomas piped up to say as he had heard the guys invite Nicky, hoping that Nicky will come with her friends and not go with these two idiots. Nicky had already decided where she wanted to go and it was to the house party, but she didn't understand why they are all not headed to the party, despite the fact she had only had the invite.

"Hey why don't we all go to the house party?" she asked Thomas and Jacob.

They had however already planned to meet some others in Herman's and so they were set on going there, they didn't want to go to the house party. Sophia comes back and is talking to the others. Matt winks at Nicky and turns his head to the side a bit, indicating for her to go with them as they were now leaving. Nicky follows them out to their car.

Thomas notices them going out by the stairs and follows too and tries to stop her but she makes a big scene swearing and cursing at him to let her go and that she makes up her own mind of what to do in life. Thomas looks on slightly anxious, slightly fuming as she gets into the car and the car drives off. The three of them, Thomas, Jacob and Sophia call a cab and head off into town to Herman's bar and continue their night without Nicky. Nicky was now sitting in the back of a car with people she didn't really know and going to a place she had never been before. She stared out the window, pretty stoned at this stage and had passing thoughts about how Richard was and what he might be up to. The car pulled up outside a typical Canadian house; wooden build, probably about thirty years old with wooden cladding around the outside painted blue but you could tell it wasn't well looked after. They walked up the short drive onto the porch and then into the house. Nicky sat herself down on the couch, there were quite a few lads wandering around the house and she noticed to herself that she didn't see any other girls around. Josh went out to the kitchen and then came back into the room carrying a couple beers for them and they sat chatting for a bit. He lines up some coke on the table and does a couple of lines, offers some to Nicky but she refuses as she's still stoned from the weed. Nicky after the car journey and the beers needed to relieve her bladder really bad, so she excused herself and went on the search for the toilet which she was told was upstairs to the left.

Washing her hands after because well, the bathroom was far from hygienic she opened the door. Josh was stood there. He makes a move on her, kissing her and grabbing her, she tries to push him away and asks him to stop. He carries on, not listening to her so she slaps him right across the face. He hits her and she falls to the floor. Immediately she regrets not staying with her friends. Things get all frosty from there, she drifts in and out of consciousness, opening her eyes to see all her clothes had been removed, and Matt was holding her arms so tight that it hurt so much. It wasn't just the punch that had knocked her out, she felt drugged. Josh was on top of her, she couldn't do anything, tears roll down her face and she eventually blacks out from the amount of drugs in her system. Opening her eyes once again, she looked down, lying naked on the bathroom floor, her body covered in bruises and blood. She couldn't quite understand, she couldn't cope with how her body was malformed, she wondered was it her, was she having a bad dream after falling asleep in the car or something. The bathroom door is shut and there's no sign of the two guys. She scrambles up a bit and manages to find some underwear to put on, though it was all ripped. She pulls her jeans up over her legs, stopping half way from the pain. She quietly bursts into tears, realising that this is no bad dream. She climbs to her feet and catches a glimpse of herself in the mirror. Her hair all messed up, with bruises coming up all over her face and she had a bloody lip and could barely recognise herself, and had no idea how long she had been there. Her thoughts suddenly switch to how do I get out of here, are those guys still here? Waiting for me downstairs? Will they let me get out of here in one piece? She sits down on the edge of the bath, sobbing her eyes out, looking down at the blood on the floor which she knew had all come from her. The door opens and in walks a girl. The girl picks up Nicky's top and helps her to finish getting dressed.

"I'm going to get you out of here" The girl says to Nicky in a very quiet voice.

Nicky was glad to hear of the help but worried as to why the girl was whispering and also confused as to where the girl had come from as she was sure there was no other girls in the house, and how did the girl know she was there? Maybe it's a trick or something but more glad for the chance at some help. They sneak quietly down the stairs into the hall way and open the front door quietly. They walk quickly down the path and the girl heckles down a taxi and puts Nicky in the car, giving money to the taxi driver. Nicky gives the driver her address and before she knows it, she is outside her home, it looked like early afternoon she thought to herself walking up the stairs to her porch. She walks in her front door, heading straight to the bed and collapses into it. Lying there, she thinks about how when she is at work as a nurse has dealt with girls coming in after being raped and starts wondering to herself what kind of drugs they might have slipped her in the pool hall. She lies there awake and then falls asleep, if it wasn't for the drugs still working their way out of her system she probably would not have slept at all.

She wakes to hear banging on her front door, she climbs out of the bed slowly and checks through the window first and sees a friendly face. Opening the door, there's a woman standing there; she has short blond hair with grey streaks in it and is wearing a loose yellow t-shirt and loose-fit dark trousers. Its Nicky's mum. She sees Nicky's face and is immediately worried. Nicky sits down on her sofa, lighting up a smoke she manages to express to her mum enough about what happened for her mum to figure the rest out. Wanting to see the guys pay for their crime, her mum asks Nicky to go down to the hospital, and to talk to the police. Nicky refuses, she doesn't want to do that. Not right now anyways. So her mum makes her a coffee and sits with her for a while. Her mum doesn't stay too long though and well Nicky wanted to be alone, wanted to try and figure this thing out in her head. She climbs into the shower, scrubbing herself, scrubbing herself to get rid of the smell of those guys and their sweat. Looking down feeling sorry for her bruised body, the bruises now coming up bright red and blue, the dried blood was now liquid again, flowing down the drain.

It's the evening, she had slept right through the day so she climbs back into bed, still not feeling herself from the drugs and falls asleep. She wakes up the next morning to the noise of her phone ringing. It's Richard, asking if she has had a good weekend. She sits there, telling him everything that has happened, and about all the bruises on her body. His heart sank. He felt useless. He knew she needed him there and he should be there to help her. Nicky reassures him she will be ok and that she doesn't want anything to change and that she still loves him. There's not much he can say except from the fact he loves her. When he gets off the phone, he logs onto his computer and gets online and searched for a flower company and arranges for a bunch of flowers and a nice card to be sent to Nicky, which will hopefully show how he cares and wishes he could be there.

From: Nicky> nicky@mynl.com
Sent: 12 April
To: Rich> richard@mynl.com
Ok well wow...yes I cried...I just want to kiss you so much right now...sending those flowers has to be the most amazing thing anyone has ever done for me...you are just wow infinity...I loved it... I love you...you make me feel so much...I can't even put this into words...I wish I could show you how I feel right now...I am just so happy...you are making me more happy than I ever could imagine right now...I am smiling ....that was beautiful...you are wonderful.. a truly amazing man...I love you I love you I love you I love you...Richard I love you... I am the happiest girl alive...God I love you so much ...I felt every word you said...I felt how much you care and how much you love me...and wow that's something eh...I love you...and now I can't do anything more than just send you this and thank you for doing something so amazing so thoughtful...I wish I could be there right now...to show you what I feel right now...cause it really is beyond words...Richard your amazing...I love you...I want to be with you forever and ever and ever...I have never experienced anything that special ever...and it

means so much to me that you would do that for me...you mean so much to me...I am just wowed...thank you so much...I love you so much...I hope you have a great sleep and a great day tomorrow...wow...I love you...mwah infinity...talk to you soon...I love you, Nicky.

Although Nicky was happy with Richard, she was far from happy in herself, she decides with all things considered, to head down to the hospital to get checked out. It was one of the hardest things in her life; she worked with these people and had to explain to them that she was there for the rape support. They examine her in a room and take detailed notes that maybe used later by the police to prosecute. She swallows the morning after pill, and they take some blood. Her blood is going in for tests, for all she knows one of the guys could have had aids or anything. How her life would be so fucked up if they have passed anything onto her. Her anger had been building for a few days now, she was feeling less sorry for herself and more furious with the guys for doing that to her. Getting home from the hospital, she's met at the door by her cousin Thomas. I guess word has got around the family a bit about what has happened. They go in the house. Thomas was furious. He saw those guys that night so he knows what they look like. He wants to kick the shit out of them. There was a rumour around Sydney about some guys that drug rape girls, in fact, the year previous these guys were rumoured to have raped a girl, then killed her and buried her body. The body had been then found by the police and it had been on the news and everything. Piecing this together in her head she started to realise how lucky she was to still be alive. Thomas leaves and tells Nicky that he will call round for her on Saturday with Jacob and pick her up. The week has been hard dealing with things and Nicky barely coped to be able to look after the kids. Although they did distract her and kept her busy, now and again she would just break out into tears and the kids had no idea about what had happened and Lauren the oldest would just come over to her and give her a hug. Friday came around and the kids went off to David's and Nicky just sat in, lit up a joint and watched a movie. She did not want to go out, what if she bumped into those guys again? Maybe they were looking for her after she had made her escape, in fact she did not feel very safe in her own house anymore.

Saturday afternoon and just as promised Thomas and Jacob show up. Getting into the car, Thomas explains to Nicky.

"We are going to find those guys, we are going to drive around until you recognise that house you were at eh" he said.

She nodded her head.

"You can stay in the car, but I'm going to sort them out for what they done to you" he said. Nicky, already full of anger had no problem with this, well as long as she did not have to see their faces. They drive off, Nicky cannot remember where the house is but remembers the general area where it was from her taxi ride, so Jacob drives off in that direction and they spend twenty minutes getting to that part of Sydney. Thomas knowing how traumatic this will be, lights up a joint and they pull in to all enjoy it with some tunes playing on the stereo. Driving off again, flash images of that night come back to Nicky as she tries to remember what the house looked like. They spend another hour driving around in vain, till just when they are about to give up and head back to Nicky's house and to the beer shop on the way.

"Turn here" Nicky says suddenly.

"It looks familiar....." she says.

Down a small path, which you could easily miss leads to a

street with about 20 houses on it.

"That's it, that's the house" she says pointing to the fourth house on the street.

Jacob pulls in close to the kerb but further up the street.

"Nicky, can you drive, keep the engine running till we come out eh" Thomas said.

The guys get out of the car, taking with them a baseball bat each from the boot of the car. A good twenty minutes go by and the lads come running out of the house.

"Drive drive!" they say jumping into the car.

Nicky pulls off, picturing in her head those guys, lying on the floor as she did, covered in blood and thinking to herself maybe there is some justice in this world, she smiled. Thomas reassures her they won't be walking for a while let alone anything else and she has no need to be scared of them anymore.

They go by the beer shop and head back to Nicky's and have light up another joint, stick on the tunes and start having a laugh and a joke. Four beers down each and they have run out, so they head around to Julia's house which is a five minute walk to the other side of the estate. She's got more beer there, and a nice bottle of vodka, and they all start getting totally slaughtered. Nicky is drowning her memories; she never wants to think of those horrible moments ever again. It gets late and Nicky wants to go home, Thomas has already hooked up with Sophia and headed off back to his place for a bit of fun. Jacob offers to walk Nicky home so she can feel safe. They get there and she asks him to stay, so she know she will be safe, so she can sleep for the night. They climb into bed and he just holds her. Nicky sleeps the whole night through and is so glad of the sleep. Waking up she lights up a smoke and chats away to Jacob. He kisses her. She kisses him back, so glad of the affection she so badly needs, they keep kissing and one thing leads to another.

From: Nicky> nicky@mynl.com
Sent: 19 April
To: Rich> richard@mynl.com
Hey what's up? so listen I am sorry but I won't be able to make it on for 2 o'clock today I am just getting ready to leave in a minute I have to go now cause I am going to take a stop out to guest home today and just drop off another resume and just see if they need anyone...I know its craziness cause I have the job I always wanted but I am a bit interested in this too..and if I could work both that would be awesome....this one I had mentioned to you before... working with seniors with mental disabilities...it would be good experience to have since the population is getting older eh....anyways I hope you understand I love you very much and I would love to be able to see you today I will be thinking about you as I always do...Richard you're so amazing...my amazing boyfriend...mwah mwah mwah infinity I hope you had a better day today...God I am going to miss you so much tonight....well I have to go for now I will catch up with you tomorrow night...I love you I love you I love you I love you infinity...hugs and kisses, Nicky.

From: Rich> richard@mynl.com
Sent: 20 April
To: Nicky> nicky@mynl.com
Hey babe, that fine about last night... I think you're mad to go and have two jobs, you'll end up with no time to yourself but maybe that's why? Anyways if it's what you want then I hope you get the job... well I'm sat here today and thinking about you and everything that's going on, I still think that maybe I should have come over to see you after everything that has happened. I know you told me that everything will be ok but it seems lately that you don't come online so much to talk to me and you hardly

ring me anymore. I know you are very busy with the kids and with your job and with the study and everything, but I want you to know that I love you and I care about you and I really hope that you are ok... I wish that I could be there. Anyways I'll catch up with you tonight when you come online...miss you xxx

From: Nicky> nicky@mynl.com

Sent: 04 May

To: Rich> richard@mynl.com

Hey what's up?...sorry I was not able to come online tonight I had to work a 3-11pm shift...I am just so crazy busy the last few days and I am sorry if it seems like I am a bit distant lately...I am still thinking about you ...I love you...I have so much on my mind besides been this busy...but you're in my mind too... you always are...Richard I missed you a lot these past couple of days...well I guess you didn't get my thing yet...cause it came back here today my mom told me when I got home...I guess I will have to find out about that tomorrow...I will call them and see what the hell the deal is with that eh...isn't that strange how yours didn't get sent here and now mine??????....bizarre....but anyways I love you and I guess all I can do is to send it again eh...I really wanted you to have it in time for your birthday...God at this rate it should be there by your 26th I suppose .... well I hope you had a good day today I was thinking about you so much today...wow I really miss you a lot...I am just laying here in bed typing this... it's much better than that awful chair...but I only have like 17mins of battery time left so I have to make this short for now...I am so tired it's like 1.00am...oh and I have to work tomorrow night at the other place... the new job out Glace Bay...and yes I have decided to go for it...so they want me to come in and work from 4-9pm... it's not too bad but I don't know if I will get online again in time to chat with you....I really do miss you...I wish you were here with me...I love you so much...well I hope to catch up with you very soon...I love you...got to go to sleep now...night, mwah infinity talk to you soon...still smiling for you...still thinking about you...I love you, Nicky.

From: Nicky> nicky@mynl.com
Sent: 06 May
To: Rich> richard@mynl.com
Ok hey what's up?...my God listen to this now will you...so
yea I was at work and this new person that just started there
today who I never met asked me to go for coffee with him...now
of course this would be no big deal if I knew them but I don't
right.:..I don't know just sitting here thinking wow eh...could be
the good hydro I just smoked but maybe not...crazy....speaking
of crazy my shift was nuts crazy busy...it was the busiest shift I
ever worked there but again maybe not eh cause at that place
counting fucking paper clips would be at light speed busy ...I
don't know I am peaking right now on this hydro little dizzy...
maybe I should say good night now ...why am I typing what I
think?...this is awesome...wow I love you...sorry about that I just
zoned out for a sec there ...weeeeeeeeeeeeeeeeeeeeeeeeeeeeee
eeeeeeeeeeeeeeeeeeeeeeeeeeeeeeeeeeeeeeeeeeeeeeeeeeeeeeeee
eeeeeeeeeeeeeeeeeeeeee....oh yea and guess what else?.......my
God what was that about...look at the e's there...a lot of fucking
e's what do you think?....this is crazy....what was saying?.....
never mind I can't remember...don't you just hate that?....oh wait
I got it....I have to work tomorrow at 12-4.00pm and then again
on Saturday from 1-1030pm...yuck yuck infinity yuck....but I am
off on Sunday ...but so what...nothing goes on here on Sunday
...half the city is off on Sundays...what the fuck eh....too many
eh's eh...boy do I ever sound like I am from cape Breton when
I am stoned....when I come over...it's getting close eh....yea so
when I come over...wait till I am so drunk then you'll hear the real
cape Breton accent ....please don't laugh though...we sound right
stupid eh....anyways there's some stuff I haven't been able to
tell you about, well so I'll just come out and say it...I have had to
drop out of school, which is why I have gone for that second job
but yea it sucks eh...I suck...but part of that is that cause I am not
going to graduate, my dad won't take me to Ireland now and that
really does suck...it makes me cry to think about it now...anyways

I got to go and chill out for a sec here....I love you Richard have a great day and I will talk to you soon....I love you so much...mwah infinity...I love you, Nicky.

From: Rich> richard@mynl.com

Sent: 15 May

To: Nicky> nicky@mynl.com

Hey babe, listen I have done a lot of thinking here about things. It's been hard coping with the fact you are not coming over here at the end of the month, because we have both been looking forward to that for so long. Anyways so what I was thinking here is that ok I have that time booked off work because I thought you would be here right? So maybe seeing as though you can't make it over here, then maybe I should come over there to you and use my holidays there with the woman I love rather than sat here for a few weeks doing nothing and missing you and wishing you was here! Anyways, have a think about it and talk it over with your friends and family and all and well I suppose let me know...I love you Nicky and miss you xxx

From: Nicky> nicky@mynl.com

Sent: 23 May

To: Rich> richard@mynl.com

Hey what's up? I love you Richard....and so I have decided...after much discussion with the family and my friends and my kids... and yes I want you to come... I seen my dad at the bar last night and he thinks that maybe it is a better idea with all other things considering...that maybe you should come here to see me...so yes please come...I need you...I really need you and I so love you....I miss you like crazy here...Ok well I am going to bed.... wish it was with you...I love you..Mwah infinity...where ever you want...talk to you soon, see you, Nicky.

Richard worries had gradually been increasing which is why he offered to go over and see Nicky during his holidays from work. Nicky had been making it online to chat less and less and had become more and more secretive, not talking about

62

things with him, and yes she was now working a lot but he felt there was more to it. It seemed as if she was drifting away from him and spending lots of her time with Thomas and Jacob but this email confirmed that she still wanted him, and wanted him there with her. Richard went into work the next day and went into his boss Liam. He sat there and asked Liam if he can have three weeks off work, Richard already have the two booked off but explained he needed the extra week as there has been some personal emergency which meant he needed to go away for a while. Liam reluctantly agrees, so Richard goes onto his own office and books flights online to go on the 30th of May for a three week trip. He didn't have much money left after that for money to live on while he is away but he had his MasterCard which he could use. It's all booked, all sorted, Richard was going to go over and make sure Nicky was ok, maybe he should have gone earlier. Richard informs his family and friends that he going over to Canada for a while for a holiday. He hasn't told anyone about what has happened with Nicky, it's not something for him to tell, it's not a piece of gossip, it was something real and something real for Nicky and he wanted her to believe that everything she said she could trust him to be confidential.

Time went by fast and it was the day before the flight. Richard was not in work that day and gets in his car and drives off to Dundrum shopping centre to pick up some new clothes for the trip. It wasn't long opened this shopping centre and this is the first time Richard had been there. He didn't stay long, Richard was one of these guys that only went shopping only if he knows exactly what he wants, what shops he can get it in and that the experience can be over and done with as soon as possible! On the way back he rings Nicky on his mobile phone.

"Hi, I can't really talk right now" she said.

"Ok, well I'm driving anyways, will I ring when I'm..."

"Yea ring when you're home" she said.

Richard thought it very weird, she sounded a bit weird. He gets home and heads up to his room with his shopping bags and the house phone and rings Nicky. Nicky answers, she doesn't say anything, Richard can make out though that she is crying, Richard guesses the words which she can't say.

"You don't want me to come now do you?" he says and he hears more crying.

"It's because you have met someone else isn't it?" he says but she still doesn't speak. "It's Jacob isn't it?" he asks.

"I'm so sorry" she says and not much more. Richard's world collapses around him listening to her sob, he can't say much except goodbye. He sits there, tears streaming down his face. 'Did I do enough?' he thinks to himself. He jumps in his car and speeds down to the off licence and fetches a bottle of vodka. Getting home and locking himself in his room, he drinks quickly, he drinks fast, beating himself up in his head of how he should have gone sooner, and he should have been there more for her. Angry with himself he throws the now empty bottle across the room smashing it off the wardrobe. He gets a knock on the door.

"Are you ok?" his brother Stephen asks from the other side of the door.

"Yea fine" he says and doesn't open the door. He lies down and sleeps it off.

Everyone deserves
Chapter5

Richard woke up the next day in the afternoon with a killer head ache. He reached for the remote control and he switched on the TV. He rolls over, unwilling to let the world see him yet. The light was shining in through the curtains; they were not lined and so after a certain time of day they do not do much of a job to keep any light out. 'I best get up then, no way will I get back to sleep?' he thought to himself. He stirred slowly, struggles to put his jeans on and, with his priorities right he stuck the kettle on and made a big mug of coffee. He was still in shock about what happened the night before and hadn't quite worked out how to tell everyone he's now not going to Canada on holiday. He flicked on the TV; no one else was in the house so he had a while to think about things, not that he was much of a mood to do so. Once his coffee was devoured he gave Rachel a buzz on the phone, and tells her about everything that had happened. So it was decided he will go to England instead for a while, well he had the time booked off work now anyways and last thing he wanted to do is just sit at home and waste his time off. He managed to get flights for that very night, the sooner the better he thought. He rang Rachel back on the phone.

"Alright English cow?" he said.

"Hi bitch boy, you stalking me?" she asked.

"Nah" he laughed "I'm just ringing ya back to say I've got flights booked and I'm coming over tonight! So like.... can you pick me up from the airport?" he asked.

"Yea what time?" she asks.

"Emm" Richard looks through his printed out tickets.

"Twenty five to nine it lands" Richard said.

"Ok I'll park at the petrol station, meet you there?" Rachel said.

"Grand, see ya later" He said.

"Ok see you later stalker" she said.

She would normally pick him up from the petrol station as it avoided her having to pay for parking at the Airport only lets you have ten minutes parking before you start being charged for being there. The petrol station is just on the other side of the car park. Richard gets his bags packed quite quickly as it was already dragging on into the late afternoon. He got a lift to the airport from his dad and explained he had decided to go to England instead as he didn't want to tell the truth. Only because he wanted to avoid too many questions on what was still a sensitive subject. He thought about the money he had lost then, those plane tickets had set him back several hundred Euros which were just gone. Maybe he should have just gone anyways, found a hotel; he'd never been across the Atlantic before. It was a choice of being alone in Canada or with his best friend in England having a laugh; well that's why he went to England. The flight over is only fifty minutes but as the plane was coming in to land he noticed something bright and glowing out the window. It looks like a huge fire, right near the airport.

As he got to the petrol station, Rachel wasn't there; instead her boyfriend was there in her car to collect him.

"Alright Mark? Where's Rachel?" Richard asked.

"Well there's a big fire down by the industrial estate and she wanted to stay and watch to see what was going on" Mark said.

"Typical!" Richard said.

Richard put his bag and his guitar in the boot of the car and they drove round to where Rachel was stood on the road bridge watching the fire.

"Hi Rachel, what's going on?" Richard asks.

"Ah I heard it's the pallet factory gone up" Rachel said.

The bridge was still at a good distance from the fire, you could not directly see the factory, but only the buildings that surround it and the flames that reached above them, and the big plume of smoke. They could hear sirens in the distance and flashing lights reflecting back as far as the bridge, but more sirens were on the way from the motorway. A couple of police cars stopped at the bridge and policemen got out, they were just keeping an eye on the spectators. Rachel's eyes drifted and noticed how close the flames were getting to the power lines. She was not the only person to have noticed, as by now there was a reasonable crowd of about twenty people including a couple of reporters with cameras. The dangerous thing was that the power lines that were so close to the flames came back along pylons towards the bridge and they had started to make some weird noises. The police moved everyone back off the bridge and just in time as the cable above the flames gave way and it all came tumbling down. It didn't hit anyone but some people were trapped on one side of the bridge with their car parked on the other side, and so they were stuck. Richard and his friends were on the good side and so they headed off back to Rachel's house. It was already quite late so they all got some sleep after the drama of the fire.

The following day the three of them head off in Rachel's car to Derby town centre. Richard had been there before, so the other two showed him around a bit. Mark had alternative motives for bringing Rachel to Derby; you see he had told her that he wanted to browse the tattoo shop as he might get a new tattoo, even though he already had eleven. However, he had no intention to get a new tattoo; instead he wanted to buy Rachel one as she had been talking about getting one for ages but didn't have the guts to do it. And so when they go into the tattoo shop, he tells her and she proceeds to pick out a Celtic design.

"Where are you going to have it?" Richard asked.

"Lower back I think" said Rachel.

"Yea so I know where to put my ash tray when we are fucking" Marks said to her jokingly.

Richard had a good look around, quite a few years before he had gone to get a tattoo, and Ann had gone with him and she spent the money on a tattoo for herself instead of him getting one. He decided to get a small Chinese symbol on his arm, as like a trial tattoo, he can always have more later at some point. Rachel is already on the table getting hers as he goes in.

"What does it feel like Rachel?" Richard asked.

"It feels like..... like a nice sort of pain" she said.

Richard is there a much shorter time than Rachel as he only gets the small one done, but the pain wasn't a problem to either of them.

"Go on then show us yours" Rachel says to Richard.

"Ha, it's tiny" she says to him as he lifts up his shirt. It wasn't that small really, but he did have big arms which made it look smaller than what it was but for quite a while he had to suffer the nick name 'tiny'. They leave town centre and head back to Mark's house for a few drinks and a barbeque. Marks sister and best friend are there, so it's a small gathering. Richard really wasn't in the mood to party anyways, he would laugh and joke and be his usual cheeky self, and then now and again his mind would drift and start thinking about things and he would get sad and feel lonely. They had just finished eating when Richard had a very strange feeling, as if he knew that something bad had happened to Nicky.

"I think something has happened to Nicky, don't ask me how I know" He said to Rachel.

"Well there's no point worrying about it, there's nothing you can do is there...." she said.

"Yea I suppose you're right" Richard said and carried on drinking his beer but took note of the time.

Richard didn't know it yet but Nicky had been in a car crash exactly at that moment, the car had been wrapped around a tree although Nicky wasn't hurt too badly. Richard spent a week in England before heading back to Ireland, and even though he was not back to work yet, he spent some well needed time with Ria to take his mind off things. When he went back to work, he had to lie about Canada, you see everyone there had expected him to be away in Canada and wanted to hear all about it. For obvious reasons he didn't want to talk about it, in case he got upset or had people laugh at him for thinking some woman three thousand miles away loved him. It was tough for a while for Richard, but he concentrated on work and Ria and his college course which he was enjoying. Time drifted past, he didn't do anything of significance or magnificence, and he just existed. Then one day, on his emails, there was a message from Nicky.

From: Nicky> nicky@mynl.com

Sent: 03 June

To: Rich> richard@mynl.com

Yea so I am just here thinking...stoned yes sir....but that's beside
the point of this...see I do my best thinking when I am stoned....
so here's what I thought up....Richard I fucked up...and wow
I really do suck...but what got me thinking was a song...yea I
think you know the one eh...so I was just sitting here listening
to it having some me time...and then it hit me....and I was like
wow yea right eh....and so I finally get it...but then I thought wait
a second maybe there is more to this ...and so I don't know if I
ever told you this but...I have tarot cards that I sometimes use if
I have really big life decisions to make...and trust me they have
never been wrong....so there I was laying the cards and here's
what they said to my answer whether or not I should send this
to you and tell you how much of a complete idiot I am for...well
everything eh....where was I one second I have to go back and
read this...be right back...oh now I remember....I laid the cards
and here is what they said...the creation of methods for the heal-
ing power of spiritual values...the gaining of respect for or from
the analyzing of long range thinking or travel......things brought to
life from the perfectionism of what is to be shared........now I don't
know about you but...wow freaked me out pretty good eh....so
I was like my god...I just made the biggest worst mistake of my
life...and I have made many mistakes...you have no idea...ok I
may see this on a different level than you might...cause well I am
high...but I also have a few secrets in the way my mind works...
and it would freak you out...but anyways...so then I was like wow
over what the cards said to me...but still even thought.. I was
like wow...I didn't know what to make of it...so I continued on by
asking what I should do about all this...and here's what the cards
said...remember the serving of people as if or they were from
god...realize the details of the philosophies and laws included...
act like a leader to what you must do and do it in a big way....then
was like fuck me eh...and so now I have to say something here...
Richard I am sorry...and wow I fucked up infinityXinfinityXinfinit-

70

yXinfinityXinfinityXinfinityXinfinityXinfinityXinfinityXinfinityXinfini-
tyXinfinityXinfinityX I am idiot X I suck X what an idiot I am....X
made the biggest mistake of my life by far X I miss you X I need
you X I love you....and there it is love....love...I really do love
you...guess I had to make the mistake to realize it...well anyways
have a good one...hope you get this...cause it made my mind
soar...alright then...talk to you soon...Nicky.

Richard didn't know what to think when he opened up his inbox and seen an email from Nicky, he let it sit there for a while and then opened it. He didn't know what to feel and to be quite honest he didn't know if Nicky deserved another chance after breaking his heart, but he did know that he still loved her. He replied to her email and says exactly that, that he does still love her, but he doesn't know what to do and maybe they should talk about things. Problem is that Nicky was pretty stoned when she sent the email, and she could barely remember sending it, and how she felt when she sent the email. Richard didn't get a reply back from her. He waited, wondering if she is ok, wondering what things are going through her mind, and thinking about if she deserved that second chance. You see deep down he knew that all this was a reaction to her getting raped. He knew at the time she would probably go a bit crazy but had never imagined things to happen the way they did. However he did understand that much about Nicky, that maybe she did love him but right now, well maybe she needs time to let her hair down, to party it up, and get drunk and stoned and whatever. In the end though she had hurt him and he was cut in two as part of him loved her still and part of him didn't like her so much for what she had done. It was nearly a month later when the two of them bumped into each other on messenger. Nicky had been out at the lake with her dad that day, it was a nice summer day there with the kids. Her dad Ethan owns a house down by the lake and a piece of land and has a big boat there too that he has

71

out on the lake during the summer months. Her dad had asked her about Richard, if she had heard anything from him. He commented how he had always made her smile. So she sat there as the kids were dangling their feet off the side of the boat, and thought about Richard and how he had done nothing but treat her right and that he really did used to make her smile all the time. So she decided that she really did want another chance at things, even though she realised it weeks before when she had been stoned. Richard had come to the decision that if she says she wants another chance that he would give her that chance, because firstly he understood why she had gone off the wall and secondly he knew he still loved her and had not felt like that with anyone else before, and thirdly because he believed in forgiveness. And so it started again, they agreed to both write a journal to keep track of what's going on and thoughts and feelings and one day we would swap them and read them. Nicky did however carry on getting stoned and partying, but Richard was ok with that because they were back together now, well not in body but you know what I mean.

From: Nicky> nicky@mynl.com
Sent: 13 Jul
To: Rich> richard@mynl.com
Well me I just ate my face off...worst munchies ever....love Billy's weed...it's so worth it....amazing stuff.....and so yea I love you eh....oh I so should have came on here a bit earlier so burning out...by the second ....need sleep...pillow fast....so gonedy...mwah I love you............
From: Rich> richard@mynl.com
Sent: 17 Jul
To: Nicky> nicky@mynl.com
Well yea....I guess I started into my journal today.....so that was cool....and I think it will be so cool for us down the line. Well I'm sitting here and thinking about me and you.... and about how I feel about you... and well I just wanted you to know that.....I

love how you are scared of bugs and one day I'll be there to chase them out of the house for you.....and I love how you get the munchies bout 10 at night because one day I will be there to make yea something to eat......and yea.....one day...we will be sat on the sofa when the kids are all tucked up in bed.....and we will just be sitting there looking into each other eyes.....with like the biggest smiles.....and wow....we cud just like spend a couple of hours kissing and cuddling while watching a movie....maybe your favourite movie...the *National Lampoon* one....or if we are getting high or pissed maybe we could watch *Without A Paddle*....but I don't think it will matter too much what we watch because we will be in each other's arms...I do love you with all my heart...and I am patient because I know that we are meant to be and I know our time will come....I believe in you and I believe in us.....When we first met we suggested that maybe I take a day off work to show yea around Dublin....maybe go for a coffee...... then we like got to the stage where we would hug......then to kiss and hug......well where are we at now? I think if we were to see each other tomorrow.....I think that we would be smiling and crying at the same time.....and definitely a big big hug and a long passionate kiss.....but that day will come one day...and I know that 100% in my heart.....I would travel the world just to see your smile .....well it's all good.....and fate brought our hearts together....it's just our bodies are playing catch up eh.....Love you xxxxxxxxxxxxxxxxxxxxxxxxxxxxxxxxxxxxxxxxxxxxxxxxxxxxxxxxxx xxxxxxxxxxxxxxxxxxxxxxxxxxxxxxxxxxxxxxxxxxxxxxxxxxxxxxxxxx xxxxxxxxxx
From: Nicky> nicky@mynl.com
Sent: 18 Jul
To: Rich> richard@mynl.com
Richard I love you so much...and I saved reading this till now... because I wanted to check out that movie first...cause I just knew that I would be too scared to watch the rest alone and so now I am kind of hearing from you now as I read your email...so it's not so bad...really wish sometimes that you were here...I mean

there are certain moments when I feel like oh I wish you were here...you know what I mean?...and hey I am going to pick up my journal tomorrow...I am taking the kids with me...there was nothing open today cause its Sunday...hey are you going to mind that when you do end up coming here...everything being closed on Sundays.....and yes it would be nice to do everything that you mentioned ...that's what I mean by oh I wish you could be here... like say I am watching something or just sitting outside or walking around the house or ...whatever ...it's just like wow something is so missing eh....and I know that it is you...you're what's missing from my life...then when I feel like that...I try to stop and just think...close my eyes and see you there with me...and it's not so bad...cause I know what I see to be true someday.... someday soon...I will be in your arms...every night...wake up every morning together...just to feel you next to me...to kiss you... to be held in your arms...would be truly amazing...and so I never stop seeing that when I miss you...and things get easier after that ...because I know that it will be real...and I believe in us too... its hard sometimes when I am talking to you on here and then when I go I wish ...oh never mind it's all good really...I miss you like crazy here....Richard...oh I have so much I want to share with you...so much I need to say to show you....and I am sorry I left like I did earlier I was burning out...I suck completely but I did have something to eat...and watched some of the movie...but you know I still thought about you and wondered if you were home in your bed dreaming about us....but hey...I love you all the same... listen I am going to meet you in my dreams right now...so until that day...and it's going to come no doubts on that...I love You...I miss you...I think about you every day and wish you were here... mwah infinity have a great day, I love you Nicky.
From: Rich richard@mynl.com
Sent: 27 Jul
To: Nicky> nicky@mynl.com
Hi babe....I miss you......well I headed down to the hospital and got there for 7.....and yeah just got home now and its after 1

in the morning...all that just for them to tell me that my knee is sprained.....but hey at least I know now for sure eh....but like I was 4 hours waiting to see a doctor....but the mad thing was because the x-ray thing is all computerised so they had my results straight away but it took them the guts of two hours just to say that you're fine ...you can go......I mean what's up with that shit?....crazy !Well how's things with you?....I hope you had a good day...sorry that I missed chatting tonight but it was out of my hands eh....I will be online tomorrow night for definite.... well you know how on Sunday night when we were having a bit of fun....and you said I haven't seen nothing yet.....well I was thinking about that while I was sat in the hospital....and I was thinking like there is sides to you and sides to me that we have yet to explore......and not just the big stuff like kissing.... making love......but also the small stuff.....like how I used to paint *Disney* characters onto kindergarten rooms.....well it's all there and waiting for us to explore.....and well I look forward to all that a lot....and look forward to sharing all my stuff with you.... but most of all I look forward to holding you in my arms....I know in my heart that you are the one......not because you are smart and sexy or because you have curly hair or because you like psychology or because you have a good heart....but because when I close my eyes and think of you I feel a warmth through my body.....a feeling so intense.....and so full of love....I know what I want right now is to be there with you....to hold you...... share life with you....have some fun.....and yes...I know that you would never ask me to do anything drastic and would leave it up to me to decide......and so I want to make you a promise..... (as long as you are ok with me making promises)......I promise that I will come over to you....my heart is yours and that will never change ever....and yea for sure when you head out on the weekends I wish I was there but seeing as though I am not.. it's good that you are still going out and having fun.....and I want you to know I am here for you no matter what it is happening in your vast mind ....or no matter what is happening in your life....I am here....just tell me.....and until I am there to be with you I will pray that God will keep his eye on you...or for him to send an angel to look after you. I know David messed you around a lot as Ann did to me but in different ways I guess but when we both met we had come out of relationships that were not so good and we had been messed about a lot I guess by people that never really loved who we were inside......and well yea I do love you for who you are.... and I know in the past there was stuff you just did not tell me.... like hiding how much weed you were doing ...but Nicky listen to me.....I love you I love you I love you I love you and anything you say or do or have done is going to change that.....

From: Nicky> nicky@mynl.com
Sent: 27 Jul
To: Rich> richard@mynl.com

Wow....ok Richard...I love you so much...and yea I am still awake...I figured I would save reading your email till after the movie cause I know I would miss you this much right now....I want you to know that at the moment those flowers came to the door...I was the happiest girl alive and when I read that card... it was so beautiful...you truly are amazing...thanks for sending flowers again...and I feel so much for you...it's amazing how you just know ...like when I am here and I think to myself that things are bad sometimes...or I just don't feel right....you are there for me...even though you are not there for me in person... just by the things you do...like little emails...or those e-cards that I just love really....or the music...and yea the flowers too.... letters...everything....everything you do shows me that you really do love me....and yea I still have some issues with trust...with good reason....and sometimes I admit I don't always take the little things that you do as a true display of your love to me... sometimes I just shake it off and say ok whatever...its true...and it's a shame...I know that...but now it's different....I can feel your love for me even more so...it's now stronger than ever before.... and I am starting to trust in that...and I am sorry for asking you the other night if you really do love me....because I know it...I know you love me...I know it in my heart and in my soul... you and me..... It's like we were just suppose to meet...like we just gel....you get me...here I will tell you something...something that no one has ever known about me...ok here it goes....hey you know what I was just going to type there just now...I was going to say don't laugh...like I use to say when I had something important to say...so I would say that...don't laugh... right before I said it... as to downplay the actually seriousness of what I need to tell you...but you know what... I am not going to say it now... see that's what I mean I am changing ...because you know what? I know you wouldn't laugh at a memory that I have that still underneath my tough presentation or whatnot... that I still think about and is of importance to me...wow I love you...ok so here it is...my secret memory one of my dearest ones as a child...when I actually was a child ...going back to about say age 5 before my parents split up...very close to when they did...but anyways....I used to play with Barbie's...yea I did...anyways...I would rehearse this little wedding fantasy...I use to get so into it...I would make them talk....I would marry these dolls...they were so much in love...I would make them kiss... make them say little nice things to each other...do you see where I am going with this yet?...I wanted to be that doll...I wanted to be her...and I hoped that one day I would find someone I could love...someone that I could trust...someone who loved me...and one day marry him...and live happily ever after....I wanted a fairy tale...I did...and I remember when I would fight with David...he would say to me ..Nicky...stop your bullshit...this is reality...life is not a fairy tale...among other things...things that made me see that he was not the one I was in need of...I could never have that with him...but anyways what I am trying to say here is that...even though over the years my life has been pretty hard...and I had to grow up a lot quicker than necessary...and lost my sense of wonder like a child...and also by being hurt I built up this wall we will call it...vowing to never let anyone in...To never chance being hurt ever again...well Richard...I must say...your love has melted the cold wall I built

around my heart...and that childhood memory never did die...
it was there the whole time...it just took a love like this to bring
it all back...and so I am ready to trust you with my heart.... I am
ready to love you with all my heart and to be loved in return...just
like the dolls...and you are the one for me...I am certain of that...
and I believe that fairy tales can be true....and my fairy tale is just
beginning...and I hope and pray that it never stops...because the
best part of a fairy tale is the happily ever after ...the part I want
to share with you...I love you Richard...goodnight...talk to you
tomorrow...I hope you feel better soon...I will be thinking about
you...mwah infinity as always...meet you in my dreams...I love
you so much, Nicky.

From: Rich> richard@mynl.com
Sent: 3 Aug
To: Nicky> nicky@mynl.com

Well I know I think a lot and I know you know I think a lot......
yea but I promise I don't worry any more.... You know when I
was up with my friend Ciara and her boyfriend on Saturday.....
me and Ciara were out in the garden with a drink and chatting...I
was filling her in on everything that has happened over the last
year and a half....and well yea was just sort of finished with
my story and well she said to me...would I have thought back
when we used to hang out as teenagers years ago if I would
ever had imagined that we would have both ended up as single
parents.....and ok she is only a single parent for another 8 weeks
because her and Daniel are getting married.....but yea it got
me thinking that my life hasn't exactly gone to plan as I seen it
would as a teen....but that's because my plan in life back then
was unrealistic ....I was focused on the wrong things.... and well
now....my plan.....well it's about building a life that's a happy
one.....and yea you are big time in my plans as you know..... but
yea I know you have some madness still to get through there
...but let me know if I am right on this ....but the other night you
nearly said something ......and then you took it back.....but I think
you were trying to say you love your weekends.....you love to

party and all....but sometimes maybe there is something else that has never been there.... that you want...and well then I sorted added one plus one again...came up with two again.....but like the way that you have never been taken out for a meal....(and mint choc ice cream...I haven't forgot that bit)...and the way that no one but me has ever bought you flowers...hmmm...so what I was thinking is that maybe that when I am there and we are doing all cool stuff together as a couple .....and no I don't ever want you to change....and I don't want yea to ever stop partying ....hope you party well into your 90s.....but maybe.... partying is not all you want from life? And yea I love to party too.... so no will we will never stop that....but I think you get what I am saying? I love you Nicky......
hugs and kisses
From: Nicky> nicky@mynl.com
Sent: 4 Aug
To: Rich> richard@mynl.com
Well yea your right about wanting more...I do...I want all that other stuff...but I still have to party a bit more first...see I am changing...no wait...more like becoming me...finally...to just be me...and see the recklessness well it's all my process...like putting myself in life threatening situations...like the car crash and hitting the tree episode or contemplating jumping off that cliff at the Indian graveyard...see there's so much more I mean by that...what I was saying was I need to finish my bullshit I do...and I am almost done...partying well...the weekends...love Fridays... but yea it would be nice to have more than just partying...I know if you were here you would be partying with me and that's cool but what's way cooler would be to come back home...to our place and just chillax...just to sleep next to you....and want so much to know the making love thing...and I want that with you....cause what's better than a party...the after party...mwah infinity I love you so much, Nicky.
From: Rich> richard@mynl.com
Sent: 4 Aug

To: Nicky> nicky@mynl.com

Well I know what you mean about all that stuff, wasn't it a freaky thing though that on the day you were in that car crash that I had a feeling something had happened right at that moment. I guess it's because the connection that we have goes beyond just the normal, like sometimes I feel like we have a connection that goes beyond explanation, kind of like what twins have where they can finish each other's sentences and they also know when something is wrong... anyways I think it's cool that we have that, and as for the graveyard thing, you have to tell me all about that one at some point, maybe tell me when I am over there eh? Ok so I am going to go now and have a shower and all and clean myself up. Talk to you soon sexy xxx miss you as always xxx

From: Nicky> nicky@mynl.com

Sent: 6 August

To: Rich> richard@mynl.com

Alright so I watched a movie wasn't too bad I am wicked tired and burnt out now....I would have just typed this on the screen but I didn't want to wake you with the beeping noise...well I am thinking right...not too sure if I want to go tomorrow with dad and my aunt's house...I am just thinking of maybe having a day where it's just me...haven't done that in a long while...and so yea I think that's what I will do besides I have a few things to think about and a nice relaxing day just doing nothing...I mean like I could just have a nice relaxing bubble bath...no interruptions...listen to music ...maybe go for a walk...just chillax all day...now that sounds amazing ...see I am always doing something...so maybe I should have a whole day just to do nothing...sounds awesome eh...just to do nothing...wow I love nothing...mwah infinity...so yea maybe if you're on sometime tomorrow night after my day of just doing nothing I will catch up with you then?...well if you can it's all good...I love you so much....I am going to have the best sleep of my life tonight I can just feel it...and it's been along long while since I had a real good sleep...well I will be dreaming of you that's for sure...miss you...I love you...talk to you soon...your

amazing...mwah infinity...oh Richard I just love you so much....
have a great day ...goodnight, mwah, Nicky.
From: Rich> richard@mynl.com
Sent: 6 Aug
To: Nicky> nicky@mynl.com
Hiya...well Ria is all tucked up in bed for her afternoon nap...
so I just watched *Without a Paddle*....I loved it...and yea
well overdue for me to have watched it....it was too funny.....
Sorry that I could not stay on longer last night but I needed the
energy here for having Ria around....And I got your email....
and I hope you have a fantastic day just chilling out and all....
sounds awesome.....I want to just say because I know how I
am....that well you know how I mention marriage and kids and
all that and coming over to live with you....it's not that I expect
things to be instantly like that....I think that for me....the most
important thing is for us just to be together.....and well everything
else will just all fit into place when the time is right....and I think
u feel like that too .....So it's all good......I love you mwah infinity
xxxxxxxxxxxxxxxxxxxxxxxxx
From: Nicky> nicky@mynl.com
Sent: 17 Aug
To: Rich> richard@mynl.com
Ok so my mom finally got back to me about immigration
information that she was getting from her friend.... not a lot she
could tell me as of yet though ....apparently Dawn no longer
works in that department anymore as of two years ago....but
anyways a friend of hers Jen does so here is what she sent
me..........
Dear Nicola:
I have some info on the visa/sponsorship deal...He may come
here as a visitor for up to 30 days or six months (can't work
during that time however. If he comes here he can apply for
"landed immigrant status" after 30 days and you do not need
sponsor him. The status for British Isles residence is not quite
as strict as say Iran or Iraq or other European countries. I can't

remember the government agency he needs to talk to I'll talk to Jen again and find out. Ok I love you, Mom.

But yea so that's not really any detail but anyways she also said to check out a site. Its http://www.immigrationexpert.com/immigration_canada.asp anyways I love you Richard and hopefully I will hear more on it tomorrow...but I just checked out that site myself and there are assessments for all kinds of different visas ...check it out until I hear more and I will let you know...god I just miss you so much right now...I watched TV for a bit...had something to eat...just have this strong feeling here... it's like I miss you but wow I love you...and it's so intense... sometimes I think about you coming here and I am just so happy...then I miss you even more eh...it's like there is always something missing...and I know it's you...Richard you have my whole heart and soul...I am so happy to have found you and I believe good things come to those who wait...and I will wait for you...cause you are the one for me...I just want to be with you...I want to share my whole life with you....since I have known you... you have done some amazing things to me....it's just like wow.. finally...and it all makes sense now...life is crazy eh...but I know since I met you my life has never been quite the same really... it's now more meaningful...it has purpose and is happier...it's amazing...you are amazing...but it's not totally complete...I know you understand what I am trying to say...which is good cause that's what I mean...me and you just gel...it is awesome...I have never in all my life felt like this...I have never been so much in love with anyone as I am in love with you...I just want to be in your arms right now....I want to show you how I feel...I want to be able to look into your eyes and tell you how much you mean to me...how much I love you....to touch you or kiss you....I miss you....have a great day tomorrow ..I will be thinking about you as I always do...mwah infinity talk to you soon, I love you so much, Nicky.

Journal Part One
Chapter6

Sun 17ᵗʰ July

Well I guess this is my first entry in the journal. This was all Nicky's idea, that we could have journals that one day we could show our kids, and I thought that was pretty cool. It will be two weeks on Tuesday since me and Nicky started talking to each other, what a beautiful crazy night that was. I mean I went to bed at like nearly six in the morning and I had to get up at seven for work. I may have been a massive wreck that day at work but I sure had a big smile, because after a couple of months apart, I found out Nicky was still as much in love with me as I am with her. Wow I missed her smile, her gorgeous eyes, and I missed how it felt knowing that she loves me. I know that at this point, I know I would have kids with Nicky, I would marry her for sure, and I would want to spend every living day to wake up to see her face beside me. But I mean all those things are massive, and because I know I would do them all right now with a fantastic girl that have never even met face to face, well some people would call me crazy, well I am crazy in love and that's for sure. It's like in my heart I can feel her here with me, and those feelings are so intense, you know and sometimes things are just so fantastic I just lose the ability to think. I said once to Nicky that our relationship will be unique and I for one would never try to squeeze it into any sort of shape just to keep others happy, and I think that now, we are breaking barriers within ourselves and within our relationship. And each day is another day shared, and each tomorrow brings us another step towards our hearts desire; just to be with each other, in each other's arms. Smiling here, but yeah sure things hasn't exactly gone to plan so far, but we are still us, miss you babe xx

Mon 18th July

Well study has to be a bit intense this week so I hope I can keep my energy levels up! I got my exam result back today and I done well, but I do wish I had Nicky here so we could celebrate. Well last night we had a bit of a laugh though Nicky had a real paranoid thing going on, so she went on to watch a horror movie, like that would help! But anyways after that she read the email I had sent her earlier on in the day, and she sent me a real sweet email, which I read when I got to work this morning. Yeah so I was feeling pretty good today to say the least, started hugging people at work and telling them about Nicky and how in love I feel. Anyways last night we sort of chatted about being together for real doing all the simple things together, and enjoying every moment together. The more I am coming out of myself the more uncomfortable I feel in this house. The last year has been a long long journey, and well the journey continues on, as I continue to face my past and deal with my future. But I am glad I chose this path, because I know things have been up and down since then but, it's on days like this I am really really glad to still be around.

I guess I had a Freudian slip today, slipped out about thinking of moving to Canada, but hey I know that it was in my head anyways. I know I will follow my heart there, I just hope to get it right, the right timing. I was also thinking today about buying a nice present for Nicky, just because, well just because I think it would be a nice thing to do.

(Later) Well I don't know, I guess sometimes it's hard at times like these when I know Nicky hasn't had the best of days and there's nothing I can do to help her out, and well yeah she ended the conversation pretty quick tonight, so I hope she is ok, last thing I want her to feel is to be there all alone, and yea for sure I know that I should be there now, in fact I would have been there right now, so it's not easy either and I don't know maybe for Nicky she knows that which isn't going to help if she is thinking constantly that I would be there now if it wasn't for the decision she made back in June, but I still love her, but I am not there to reassure her, and that's hard for me.

Tues 19th July

Well I'm glad I'm not a cat tonight because curiosity would have killed me. Well I guess the other day I went looking for details on college courses over in Canada, because well just as I need to know information for my head. And well tonight I was browsing on the internet and went onto a couple of immigration web sites, I know it might yet be a bit early to be thinking like this or maybe not, but anyways I can came across a snippet of information, which was that Nicky could sponsor my immigration to Canada, as long as a long term relationship for over a year, so yeah, nice bit of information for me to think about. Well I'm quite excited to talk to Nicky tonight because I missed her today, there's a lot of things that always seem to pop up that just remind me of her, and well I hope she's feeling a bit better today too.

Wed 20th July

Well last night was one of those fantastic nights again; we had a great chat and a great laugh. Nicky was just strolling about in her knickers, and had been all day, even out in the garden. It's like 40 degrees over there at the minute so it's very very hot, we don't exactly get it that hot over here. Em I met one of Nicky's aunts last night... well sort of seen her enough to say hi anyways, and Nicky then filled her in that we are back together, and well she's very supportive so it seems, so that's cool. I also got a good glimpse around Nicky's place, she had her laptop in the lounge so she showed me around a little, yeah and it looks good, though

I know it would look a lot better if I was there in person. It also turns out the tape of music I sent Nicky last week arrived there yesterday, and I had sent a card for Gavin's birthday too, so Nicky said she was crying again listening to the songs I wrote for her. Apparently Lauren was asking when I am coming over and whether I could teach her a song or two on the guitar. So my heart melted a little bit more eh, I mean life here is just, well it's just an existence for me at the moment, apart from when Ria is around, or when I'm talking to Nicky or one of my friends. It is pretty isolated, and well I only ever returned here to Ireland last summer because I missed Ria, but I still only see her every second weekend, which works out as like 52 days a year, which really does suck, and well I love her to bits and think she's as crazy as me. Well I do love having Ria around, and for sure I would have more kids with Nicky, and for sure my life doesn't seem complete right now, and that's because Nicky isn't here beside me every day, but I guess we have all that to look forward to, so it's all good. Well I guess I know I think a lot, and what I was thinking was that maybe the reason I have not been able to build a proper life here for myself is because this is not where I am going to end up staying at, well anyways, got to go.

Thurs 21st July

Last night was fantastic, we chatted till half three in the morning. Yea we like to talk and make up words and smile at each other, and yea even last night Nicky was crying, but they were happy tears. I think last night we mentioned it but it had been on my mind that even though it does not seem possible, but, somehow out of this we have become a lot stronger, a lot happier and a lot more in love, and that's for sure. I think marriage was mentioned again last night, but it's all good, and I love Nicky a lot, so yea mentioned my big plan to her last night, and also she told me cool stuff about how she reckons the song I wrote for her is one she has been humming for years, before she even knew me, and yea the tape I sent over is causing a bit of squabbling between Nicky and Lauren, they all want a turn to use the tape player. Well I guess I do feel loved and I know I love Nicky, so yeah, marriage, kids, old age, and mid-life crises too I suppose. I want to be with Nicky for it all. Bring it! Empty house tonight, parents are off up north to a wedding, and Stephen is at work, so I spoiled myself, I cooked pasta and sweet and sour chicken, but the chicken was breaded. OMG it was fantastic, and had to have a couple of drinks to finish it off. Well it's a happy day, and I hope Nicky is doing well; I am looking forward to chatting to her in a while.

Fri 22nd July

I was glad to catch up with Nicky briefly when I got home from work. Maybe she sensed I needed a quick hello and knew I was online right at that moment because I only came on for 10 minutes to burn a CD to listen to when driving down to collect Ria, and to check my emails.

(Later) I just finished watching *Titanic*, what an intense and sad film, for two people to find love like that and then to lose him wow... so sad even though I have seen it before. Well I'm sitting here and I miss Nicky a lot today, I think it's just one of those days where I couldn't understand why I am not just over there with her now. I seem to be having a lot of dreams recently, like a huge amount of dreams about a lot of different things, I took a glance at the plane tickets to Canada that I booked back in January, and well I'm quite sure what my decision is going to be. In May, I could not risk being in a country thousands of miles away from my friends and face the biggest heart break of my life. So yeah, Nicky had told me not to go, but part of me always wishes I should have gone anyways, so this time around, I reckon, if I do this, I am going no matter what happens, I would not take such risks if I did not believe that this is all worth my effort, I must keep my heart open, and my mind focused. I miss Nicky a lot here, but she's out partying and I love her and trust her and believe that she loves me. When Nicky used to ask me 'why were you not born here', I always answered, because God has a sense of humour. Well maybe it's time to pull in a favour, a man with faith is a powerful thing.

Mon 25th July

Well I guess I had a busy enough weekend with Ria, studying hard whenever she was sleeping because I got an assignment to do this week for college. Well I missed Nicky a lot over the weekend, sometimes I pray to God and ask him to look after her until I can be there. At the minute I am listening to a song Nicky sent me called *'God bless the broken road'* and wow very wow song, it's my *Rascal Flatts* but wow infinity. So anyways me and Nicky caught up with each other last night after the weekend, she had a pretty crazy weekend, Friday night at some haunted cliff, and Saturday at a wedding and of course Gavin had his party yesterday too, but anyways we had a pretty cool chat last night, we was going to head to bed bout 2.30 am but still stayed talking till like 4am, it's all good and I'm getting used to it now, so we had a lot of a 'I go > you go' fun, which was right cool, then we tried a video conversation, Nicky could hear me but I could only make out some of what she was saying, but wow how I have missed her voice, was pretty cool to hear her again. I suppose my phone bill will go mad again when Nicky gets her phone reconnected, but I am looking forward to it big time, though obviously not as much as I am to actually being over there with Nicky and holding her in my arms...finally. Catch you later.

Wed 27th July

What a crazy day I had yesterday, I mean a stupid accident at work which left me crying with pain but laughing because it was funny. So like I was driven home and dropped off and I put frozen vegetables on my knee to stop the swelling, then at like 6 o'clock I bumped into Nicky as I was writing an email, that seems to happen all the time now, but anyways, I felt like I should head down to the hospital and ended up stuck there till one in the morning. I didn't bring anything to read, but that was kind of on purpose, so I could have a little time to think. And so I sat there thinking about good things that lie ahead, so it was good to give time to myself to let all that out. So when I got home I was sat at the computer typing out a nice email, when Nicky came online, and she had got the flowers I sent her, and we had a nice chat, we talked about down the line a bit and caught up with each other, and I can't wait to see her tonight, really really really looking forward to seeing her. Also Nicky sent me some stuff last Thursday, so can't wait to get it, I think some of the things she might send is from way back in April. Well I am doing well today, apart from my knee which is quite sore, and I have to catch up on my study so, off I go.

Thurs 28th July

What rubbish weather, you kind of get used to summer but today it is cold and rained all day long, you should have seen all the depressed faces at work today, it was crazy. I had a stressful morning, but yea things were sure better by the time I was heading home, I was feeling pretty good actually, so I cooked something quick> pasta, and got stuck into my assignment and got a good bit done, so I'm not as stressed out as what I was last night which is good, well I don't like stress, stress and me are not good friends. Well waiting on the edge of my seat till this stuff arrives from Nicky, I know

I am going to write her a nice letter this weekend and there's some music I want to send over to her. I think today was like a trial for me and my feelings because well I think that May has haunted me a little, and yeah I feel ready to let all that go for sure. It's not that I've ever doubted Nicky or how we feel, it's just that I suppose I was just being a little careful but I don't need to be now, I have confronted that ghost and sent it on its way, and well let's bring this thing called fairy tale, and this thing called love, and this thing called us. Nicky you have my heart, I love you so so much, and I will do whatever it takes, I am coming over to you, and one thing I noticed today and that's how we used to count the days till when we meet and we don't do that any longer because well we are more confident and just know that this is coming, and fate has brought us together, so time no longer matters, for sure I would love her to be here now, but timing for when we get together does not change the fact that it's going to happen for sure.

Mon 1st Aug

Well what a crazy busy weekend, at least I got my assignment finished, and yeah went up to see Ciara for a few hours which was cool. I missed Nicky a lot this weekend, and I even wrote her a massive email bout things and I'm sending her a letter in the post tomorrow with a few little things.

Well I'm just going to chill out here a little and wait for Nicky to come online and yeah I've decided to do a road trip all the way around the coast of Ireland, which is about 1500km but I'm looking forward to that. Also I sent off for info about doing parachute jump which I know I would love to do as well. Last night I had trouble sleeping, I just missed Nicky so much, and I was tossing and turning all night, and when I checked my emails today, it turns out Nicky had not slept so good either. Well got to go have a quick shave and all before Nicky comes online, and I have a little surprise for her tonight if she's up for it, fingers crossed eh.

Tues 2nd Aug

Yea so last night was another late one, was up till about half five in the morning. Em so like I wrote things across my chest in permanent marker for Nicky, also I managed to leave my web cam on all night so Nicky could see me in my bed asleep. Well the October trip was mentioned a little too, about me going over, Nicky was maybe having a little doubt about whether I would come or not. Well what's a man supposed to do when the girl he loves lives so far away? Hey you should see the state of my pillow from where the marker sort of came off while I was sleeping.

I know that I am going to head to Canada. I put hope that Nicky will be there with her arms open when I do. Got to try a couple other things tonight, I love Nicky, and want to be with her, fate fate fate fate fate fate.

Wed 3rd Aug

Well last night was cool; we had a nice chat, though Nicky took ages before I could see her smile because she was a little paranoid last night but definitely worth the wait for sure. Well last night was the second night I left my webcam on going to bed, and last night I was really really missing Nicky like mad. I was nearly crying and everything. When I got into bed and closed my eyes and dreamed and I went back to that place and I seen her by the lake, and it was like I started seeing myself in another place, and it was like both places just came together as if our paths together are written in the stars. When I woke up for work I was writing a little message for Nicky on messenger, and as I was writing, I got one from her saying I love you, which was very very cool, because it was like four in the morning over there and turns out she gets up at that time every night for a smoke. Well when she told me that something inside was telling me that when she lies in my arms in bed, I don't reckon she will, because she will feel safe, loved and happy, and no I don't reckon I'm anything special, but I guess if Nicky is in love with me as I am with her then I think we will both just be complete when we are finally together.

Also Nicky said last night bout still needing to go a little crazy, still, which is cool, I need that too sometimes, though I tend to go from one far extreme to the other and back again, that's just me I suppose. And yeah Nicky is Nicky, and she needs what she needs and I love her, so her needs are important to me.

This is the most chilled out night I have had in a long time. I'm looking forward to having Ria on Friday, might take her down to Wicklow if the weather is good, also have a free gaff for two weeks from Friday on as the parents are away, which will be cool, though I will have to remember to wake up in the mornings, two days in a row now that I have slept in, ah well, fuck it.

My mind started thinking about something today, about October; because I know once I am there I am not going to want to return, so I will make a backup plan in case I decide to stay. I mean my plans now stand at going over for two weeks, coming back, sort out financial stuff here and then go back over with a visa and stuff, though I don't think I am being realistic with myself here because I know I will be tempted to just stay forever, so I will have two plans ready, and we'll see what happens. It's all good either way. In fact when I think about it, Stephen might take my car off my hands and the payments, saves me selling it! And well would just have to deal with the other bill, and yeah also I will have to have a long chat with Ann and sort things out about Ria.

Anyways I'll let my mind think all about that for a while. I think the road trip is it, it's when everything in my head will just slot into place and then I will just go for it.

I Promise
Chapter 7

From: Nicky> nicky@mynl.com
Sent: 27 August
To: Rich> richard@mynl.com
I love you I am so sorry I mean didn't plan to go that quickly or
come back this late...see the whole town is dry of weed right
so I had to go over Julia's make a whole bunch of calls cause
Thomas was fresh out right ...then I get drink with my aunt cause
Thomas went to the bar with his girlfriend and I just wanted some
weed and to be honest here I sort of would have went then I
thought about you fuck I am so high right now but I mean Richard
if you have to feel love you should feel it when your high its holy
fuck I am so high eh.....I love you that's the point I am seriously
trying to make here and I didn't want to go because I wanted to
talk to you and so I am home now missing you and I am so sorry
but after all that see here's what else happened...tripped me right
the fuck out here...like holy shit...I couldn't get weed and I was
watching the clock in the kitchen I was like I need to get some
fucking dope here man and go talk to Richard...now here's the
trippiest thing ever in my whole long years of being stoned ever...
infinity here's what my aunt said wait I will get you some I know
just the fella to call...so she calls this fella which actually turned
out to be one of my ex's dads???? I know what the fucking
chances of this mad unbelievable shit happening eh ....anyways
then he says like the town is dry man...I am like so I have heard
he goes but for you darling I would...I was sure then so he goes
up to the horse track brings it back the whole time Thomas was
like I give it 50 /50...that the guy would come back and deliver it
to the house just for us eh...Thomas was freaking out the entire
time....I will tell you why in minute this whole night has been so
trip out...anyways I will tell you the rest if you sign on but really

94

I am just home now had a real FUCKIN TRIPPY NIGHT MAN
my family is more fucked then I had thought...I mean fuck, trippy
shit....anyways the point of this whole thing Jesus did I write that
much yea I fucking love you true story and everything...MWAH
hope talk to you soon...Nicky.
From: Nicky> nicky@mynl.com
Sent: 27 August
To: Rich> richard@mynl.com
I love you please come back...I miss you...I am sorry ok I should
have mentioned it before when I say a time I mean give me
an hour after that time cause well I suck ..kind of like my dad
in a way he doesn't even own a watch...so yea I am late very
sorry I miss you so much thought trippest night of my live my
family is awesome...*Sopranos* haven't got nothing on us...true
story and everything...I love you please come on I have a good
explanation...ok this is just weak....I must love you eh...I love you
Richard...talk to you soon...mwah
infinity Nicky.
From: Rich> richard@mynl.com
Sent: 28 August
To: Nicky> nicky@mynl.com
Hey babe, its morning and I'd thought I'd just come online and
check my emails, and there was two waiting there from you.
Sorry I wasn't online last night to chat, well I was on earlier in the
night but I went to sleep pretty early so missed you I guess when
you came home. Anyways I hope we can catch up later and you
can tell me the rest of story eh? Talk later sexy xxx love you xxx
Rich.
From: Nicky> nicky@mynl.com
Sent: 29 August
To: Rich> richard@mynl.com
Hey what's up?...I love you too so much Richard...I am still
not asleep I downloaded a movie I watched that and now I am
starting to get tired...I miss you a lot....Richard when you come
here my whole life is finally going to begin...I mean my fairy tale

come true...I have spent so much time just dreaming of this...I am just so happy...it's amazing.. I really can't find the words to express everything I need to tell you...but I will show you...I am going to love you my whole life with my whole heart and soul forever and ever infinity...I would love to be lying in your arms right now...you mentioned the cuddling thing before and you know what I want that too. I want all that stuff....you mean everything to me....I love you...meet you soon I am going to get some sleep...I miss you I love you mwah goodnight and have a great day today....love you, Nicky.

From: Nicky> nicky@mynl.com
Sent: 12 September
To: Rich> richard@mynl.com

Hey what's up? well I didn't make it to school this morning my dad forgot to pick me up so anyways then we got in this huge fight....I am just a mess now....sometimes I just feel like nothing ever works out eh...I will be ok...really feel like just giving up sometimes....I really wanted to go...I was all ready and I had the kids ready...then he didn't show up...I have a feeling that things this year in regards to school and that are just not going to work out...like who I am kidding I can't do this....I just wish that for once in my whole life that someone could be there for me to maybe depend on eh....it's just hard sometimes to do what I want to do what I need to do...I knew ever since David left that things would be hard...but this is ridiculous...this happened to me last year too... see I ended up dropping out of some of my courses because I had problems finding people to watch Gavin and trying to get Lauren to school in the morning...and I was just destroyed over the David thing....I would ask David to help me out some and he would never show up....but every day I just kept trying to live my life...and now today it just sucks....I mean its only one day right but then it turns into two days and so on...I beginning to think maybe I should just forget about it....alright Richard so you wanted into my head well here it is...I have been let down far too much by people in my life that said they would be there

for me people that said they loved me...people that said they
wanted the best for me and those same people are the ones
that never come through for me....then dad has to bring up my
mother...saying how mom never does anything for me...and he is
right about that...but then when he said I have to learn how to do
things for myself....well that was it...I lost it....I have been doing
everything for myself since I was a child...I had to watch my
sister when my mom worked two jobs....I never got the chance
to be a child....I was cooking and cleaning by age 6....I can't stop
crying....might be cause of the weed but maybe not...I just feel
so awful right now....I love you...and Richard what I love about
you the most is the fact that you mean what you say when you
say it an even though you are not here right now....I know you
will still be there for me somehow...you are amazing....I am sorry
see I don't want to bother you with my crazy life....I wish I could
hug you right now.....I am not going to that interview either...I am
not doing anything today hopefully it will be better tomorrow....I
hope you have a good day....and don't worry about me I am ok...I
still have a pulse eh...maybe I don't deserve happiness....maybe
I am suppose to just be like this for the rest of my life...maybe
I will never be anything special and maybe I don't deserve you
either....I have to go Gavin wants me...I need to stop crying....I
love you....Nicky.
From: Rich> richard@mynl.com
Sent: 13 September
To: Nicky> nicky@mynl.com
Hey babe, I am so sorry you had a bad day yesterday... it sounds
like you had a bit of a breakdown there and I wish I could have
been there to give you a nice hug. Well listen when I come over
and I know it's still weeks away, but when I am over there then I
will help out, you know look after the kids whenever you need me
to and help get you to school or whatever, I want to be the part
that makes everything right for you and be that person that you
can lean on and depend on for anything, and I know I try my best
from here but on days like that it's not enough and I just wish I

could be there for you. Hope you are having a better day today and sure even if you are not having a good day, I'll meet you online later and get you smiling again ok? I promise everything will be ok xxx I love you xxx Rich.

From: Nicky> nicky@mynl.com
Sent: 14 September
To: Rich> richard@mynl.com
I love you so much....mwah infinity you are amazing...ok well I have to go and walk Lauren over to school then come back here and get a shower and get ready....then at 11 I am leaving here.... so maybe I might get a chance to come on when I get back cause I really need to have a coffee here when I get back...I love you so much....ok talk to you soon...I miss you...I can't wait to be able to kiss you when I wake up and have a coffee with you...tell you how much I love you...Richard I love you so much...Nicky.

From: Nicky> nicky@mynl.com
Sent: 14 September
To: Rich> richard@mynl.com
Hey what's up? miss you like crazy...but it's all good I will talk to you tomorrow eh...I hope work was well as good as work can be...and I hope you had a great day...I am just on here now trying to find a book I need for class ...I have to order it through the library...anyways...other than that just thinking about you miss you and I am so in love with you...Richard...I promise I will not tell you not to come this time...I am still very regretful for telling you the last time not to come believe me this time it's not going to happen...I love you so much...I need you I want you forever and ever....so have no worries on that...mwah infinity everywhere...I can't believe I am this tired...I had a long day...then I had Thomas and Sophia over for supper...I had barbecued pork chops and mash potatoes and mixed veggies and baby corn...it was very good...I was so full it was ridiculous...but I guess that's what happens when you don't eat for a while eh...I came home today at around 4 and I was starving ....anyways ...I wish you were here

more and more and more and more everyday...I love you more and more and more and more every day....well if you come on I will talk to you later if not I miss you and I love you and I will talk to you soon...my class tomorrow is from 4-7 so I won't get able to get online till say 8...but I love you all the same eh...alright well love you Richard....so much...mwah infinity everywhere, Nicky.

From: Rich> richard@mynl.com
Sent: 15 September
To: Nicky> nicky@mynl.com

Hey babe, well I guess it has been something that has been on my mind, I'm sure you can understand that I still have some fears because of how everything went last time, and it's nice to hear those words that you won't tell me not to come, I think on some level I needed to hear you say it...and I know you are sorry for last time and I have forgiven you because I do love you with all my heart. Anyways I know you won't be on till later than normal tonight so yea I will be here, looking forward to seeing you and I hope your day at work has gone ok xxx love you lots xxx and miss you lots xxx

From: Nicky> nicky@mynl.com
Sent: 18 September
To: Rich> richard@mynl.com

Hey what's up? Good morning....I love you....I missed you too...oh my God I got so scared when the lights went out last night....I came back here like an hour after I was talking to you I was so stoned and then I was just sitting here going to watch a movie and then it was just total black out ....anyways I found some candles and anyways when it came back on I think I left you something on here...I was going to put my cam invite on before I watched the movie then it was gone again....this time the connection....then I just got so burnt out and I must have fell asleep and here I am I miss you...I was going to send you an email last night too. I read the e-card you sent me I loved it...I love you so much Richard....I had a good dream too and I remember a bit of it....well see you were here and the power

went out and I freaked out but it was ok because you just came up behind me and whispered in my ear that everything was going to be ok....then you started kissing me and touching me so gently and you were just so good to me....then you turned me around and we kissed some more...it was so dark but I could see you... then you took off my clothes and I helped you with yours and I could feel you naked against me...there was nothing said ...it was just so intense....and we made love right there up against the wall...you said you loved me and told me that you would always be there for me no matter what....I have never had any dream in my life that real anyways I just woke up now and I am having coffee I think I am going to think about this most of the day....I miss you and I love you so much Richard....I hope your having a great day with Ria today and I will talk to you soon...it's so windy out right now...and the rain caused a bit of damage in the living room...on one of the walls the paint all bubbled out cause the ceiling was leaking.....anyways it's all good I am ok and I love you mwah infinity love you so much talk to you soon Nicky, peace.
From: Rich> richard@mynl.com
Sent: 18 September
To: Nicky> nicky@mynl.com
Hey babe, wow your dream sounds amazing...hmm can't wait to do all that stuff for real, it will be amazing for sure...I am just finished having coffee myself, I can't live without coffee in the morning haha...So like what's the story with your roof, is it leaking real bad? Is your dad a roofer by any chance ha, only joking, I hope it's not too bad...and I hope you can get it fixed eh...Well I'm not quite sure what to do today...I might sit down and play my guitar for a bit, I think it's been a couple of weeks now since I've even picked it up. Hey you know I think I will bring my guitar over with me to Canada, who knows I might be able to get a couple of gigs around the bars and well I'd like to play some songs for you in person...ok well I'll talk you later babe xxx I love you xxx
From: Nicky> nicky@mynl.com
Sent: 29 September

To: Rich> richard@mynl.com
Hey what's up? Hope your having a great day...I am just having
a coffee here then I am going to do some more of the kitchen...
I am going to take the day off today...so I should be on the usual
time...I miss you so much...last night when we were on here...
well I mean it happens all the time....but last night it was more
intense than before...I just love you so much Richard...I promise
to show you how much everyday when you come here for the
rest of my life....I want so much to share everything with you...
and it's all going to happen soon eh....sometimes I sit here and
think I am dreaming...cause really I have never known a love
like ours...I have never felt this way in my entire life...sometimes
I think wow is this really happening....it's so amazing....you are
amazing....I think about you all the time....and all I can do is smile
even though I miss you and wish you could be here...I smile all
the same cause I know in my heart that we will be...and then I
realize that I am not dreaming... that it is real....in all this time
that we have talked on here...and even when we didn't talk for a
while...you were always there...you were always in my mind and
in my heart...that feeling...that amazing feeling never went away
it only grew into something so strong it could not be denied...and
so now nothing will stop it...I believe we are meant to be...and I
know you feel the same way...I feel that together we will be so
strong....when I think of you being here all I can do is just be so
happy....all I can see is good things to come...I have no doubts
about us ....I cannot describe to you in a way with words cause
it seems like no words will ever be able to explain something
so amazing....but I will show you...I will show you every day....I
promise....I love you Richard... have a good one...talk to you
soon...mwah infinity Nicky, peace.
From: Rich> richard@mynl.com
Sent: 02 October
To: Nicky> nicky@mynl.com
Hi Nicky.....
Well what a weekend I have had here. I didn't think it possible

but I still miss you more and more everyday.....but I have to say when I am missing you....it's not sad.....you see sometimes when you miss people....you can be sad.....but I miss you but I am still happy....it sort of contradicts itself kind of.....but it's like I can be sat there and thinking about you because I am missing you....but I have a smile on my face because I just love you so much. I know you can feel in your heart how much I love you and care about you.....and I can't wait to show you how I feel for you..... you are amazing to me.....there just are no words to describe how deep my love runs for you....I love you and I tell you I love you all the time but it's just so much more than that......I love you so much Nicola. I love you.....I love your smile....I love your eyes....your hair....I love how you have 2 cups of coffee in the morning.....I love how you only have breakfast on a Saturday.....I love how your hair looks when you have just woke....I love that you drool in your sleep....I love how smart you are.....I love your sense of humour....I love how you make me smile all the time....I love how you make me feel alive on the inside. I need you in my life.....I need you because you make my life and my heart complete. I want you....I want you because I love you so much for who you are....inside and out.....I think you are so sexy....I mean that.....you turn me on so much.....you are amazing....but I don't just want you because you are sexy.....when I say I want you..... it's so much more......because I want to share this life with you....I care about you so much....I care about what you want and need in this life...whether it be just to make you smile ...... or whether that be just a hug.....or whether it be to make love to you.....or even if yea just need someone to get you some smokes....I care about your needs Nicky.... I love you so much......and see after me saying everything I have said here.....I still love you more than all that....because there's is no words to describe how I feel....

Hugs and kisses infinity
Rich
Xoxoxoxoxoxoxoxoxooxoxoxoxoxoxoxooxxooxoxoxoxoxoxoxox

P.S. everyone else calls me Rich but I love how you call me
Richard....mwah
From: Nicky> nicky@mynl.com
Sent: 03 October
To: Rich> richard@mynl.com
Hey what's up?...ok just wow....Richard you are amazing...I love
you....alright so I am so high right now...but you know what's
funny about that...see I am high right so usually when I am high
what happens when I feel emotions it's like more intense....but
here's the thing...see whenever I am feeling those emotions...the
most amazing feeling I have ever known...loving you Richard...
is the most intense feeling ever. I mean ever...like when I am not
high...and I am talking to you its far more intense than when I
am high ...just loving you...is the most intense feeling I have ever
known...physically what I am feeling right now is just wow....and if
you were here...my God...I want you so much....I wonder if when
we make love...what these emotions are going to be like...I think
about stuff like this I really do...so I cannot even try to begin to tell
when I think about making love to you...wow....see even as I type
this I am just thinking and I just zone right here...I do this a lot...
it's like I see me and you...I can see it happening and its real...
and that's all I can type is wow...wow I love you Richard....ok so
where was I ...see I just did it again...the screen saver thingy
came up...I must have been just gone for like ten minutes...was
awesome awesome trip....Richard you are amazing...ok so what I
am getting to is I am trying to describe how I felt after I read what
you sent me...wow....Richard...I love you so much....I sometimes
think that wow Richard you are the one my soul mate...then I
read this and I am like...just wowed...it's like everything I was just
thinking about during the week was just answered by you right
there...it's like you just know...but it's like I already know that you
know and you tell me what I was wondering but it's like I know
that you are going to tell me somehow....so sometimes even
though I am thinking about me and you and wondering just stuff
right...it's like I don't bring it up...I don't ask you about what I am

thinking...because I know that somehow you will tell me...and you do....like in this email that you sent...you reassured me about a few things...things I have thought about....you are trying to tell me how much you love me...and just like me...if I was to try and do that it would be impossible...because like I said it's just too intense to describe...but you always find a way to let me know that you really love me...and I do feel that love... it's amazing... you are amazing...and all this.. all of it...not just this email that's not what I mean but...I mean the whole feeling of love and being in love with you and feeling that you love me right back is how I know you are the one...how I know you are my soul mate...and I know this because I feel it and I feel it because it just is...because we are the same...because I know that you are part of me...I believe that me and you are meant to be together and always will be...and so I just let it be from the very start...I just knew.... everything I ever wanted and waiting for was you...everything that I ever missed or did or experienced in my life ...or even all the stuff I ever fucked up was all for a reason...it was for the moment I would find you and fall so much in love with you and find my way back to you even cause who knows I don't think this feeling of love for you is something that just happened...its more intense that that it's like something that was being continued but better or stronger...like I knew you more than just for this life time...and just the other day or whatever and we were talking and you said when you think about talking to me it's like we have known each other forever right? Well that's what I mean I believe that...I just know that it is true...so in fact maybe we found each other again...soul mates forever....when I look back at so many things like when we first started talking on here well even before that...just things in my life...it was like I was ready for you...and I knew this but I just didn't know if I would find you... and then it happened and that first time we talked I just knew... you are everything I have ever wanted and wished for and waited so long for...but all that time...all that time my whole past is just meant to prepare me for what I knew would happen...I am sorry

if this sounds like the most fucked up thing you have ever heard but really....since I have been getting high again...I see things so much clearer...see my feelings for you are more intense the most intense feelings ever ..but when I am high...it's like understand it all so much more...it's not that I feel it even more but it's so much clearer...and sometimes it trips me out cause I am like wow...you really are my soul mate...and I just know....I tell you the things I have discovered in my heart and in my mind while high is just the most amazing things ever...and then when I am not stoned it all remains...I can remember feeling all this...and I love you so much more because I know you are the one...see I also believe that being high is the gate way to the unconscious mind too... so it's like my love for you is both in my unconscious mind and in my conscious state but it's also in my heart both literally and spiritually...cause I physically feel it and I feel it on another level of awareness too...like spiritually I feel it too ...alright I must be sounding like what the fuck by now so...anyways you will see when we smoke a joint together and if you feel all this stuff that I am trying to say to you here...then it will be like wow it's all really happening even though I know right now that me and you are meant to happen...when you can see it how I see it...but for some reason it's like right I just got this feeling like I am typing stuff you already understand...God when me and you smoke a joint together and take that trip together...holy wow...Richard I have never in my life been able to feel this much this intense this real this amazing in my whole life...I love you...on so many levels...I love you...mind, body and soul...alright I still never ate here I need to get something to eat....Richard I love you...and I love your name...and soon I can whisper your name...Richard I love you.. in your ear when I am on top of you...and I can feel you deep inside me...oh Richard...Richard I love you....mwah infinity talk to you soon,
Nicky, peace.
From: Nicky> nicky@mynl.com
Sent: 03 October

To: Rich> richard@mynl.com

Ok so what's up? I had a great sleep last night...I love you...I am home for the day today cause when I went in to wake up Gavin this morning he is sick again...it's just unreal...it seems like every time he starts to get better after he gets home from being with David he is sick again....anyways he has a fever and his voice is kind of crackly...I gave him a chest exam myself because well I know how to do that...but anyways he has a lot of consolidation in his lungs more on the left side than the right and it's in the lower portion of the lung so what I am going to do is take him up to the hospital because I am thinking that maybe it is not a cold... see when David was younger he had asthma...so I am thinking Gavin may have that as well...it is possible but I am hoping he doesn't...anyways right now I am just having a coffee then I am going to get dressed and take him up....I hope you are having a great day...I miss you... I love you so much...talk to you soon... mwah infinity everywhere....I love you, Nicky, peace

From: Rich> richard@mynl.com

Sent: 05 October

To: Nicky> nicky@mynl.com

I love you so much.....I hope you do great in your test today and I hope you are not feeling sick when you wake up.....if I was there and you were sick I would take care of yea promissinfinity.... and if I got sick too, well I would be extra horny, so we would be in bed (wink wink) until we recover. I was walking into work today..... and I was thinking about me and you walking around the mall in Halifax....doing some shopping....but we had these huge smiles on our faces.....and we were holding hands.....and every now and again...we would just stop browsing the shop windows.....turn and look each other in the eye and kiss....I really really love you so much.........and I miss you more and more.......I think it's awe-some that we chat on the voice messenger thing now because I love talking with you and well the typing thing has to go soon eh.......it will go when we can talk and see each other at the same time.....in about 23 days....well I hope you have a good day....I

will be thinking about you all the time.... I love you so much
Nicola......talk to you later tonight.....hugs and kisses infinity xoox-
oxoxoxooxoxoxoxoxoxoxoxoxooxoxxooxxooxo
Rich
P.S. one more day gone.....another day closer mwah
From: Nicky> nicky@mynl.com
Sent: 05 October
To: Rich> richard@mynl.com
I love you Richard...just having my first cup of coffee here....I
tried to read last night I got to the third page I crashed right on
top of the book...I woke up again at 11 and Julia was at the
window yelling to me so I got her what she wanted all half asleep
and then went back to bed my clothes were still on by the way...
and I never woke till 8 this morning....crazy eh.. I was so tired...I
didn't even put the webcam on for you, sorry about that...I miss
you I love you I hope you are having a great day... and I feel
alright today ...I feel a little weak and my throat is still sore but
other than that I am fine for now....I love you so much and I can't
wait till you come it's going to be awesome...and you know I just
pictured every word about us in Halifax and wow....I love you so
much...there is nothing I can say to something that seems so
simple eh...like holding hands in a shopping mall...although it is
something so simple it's also something I want to do with you...
and so it's amazing...it's all amazing you are amazing Richard
and I love you...forever and ever....so have a great day and yea I
will talk to you soon....mwah
infinity...I love you, Nicky, peace.

Journal Part Two
Chapter8

Sat 6th Aug

 Wow I feel so tired right now, most of this week I have been
up late talking to Nicky with the exception of last night but
I still managed to wake up in the middle of the night to have
a chat with her. Nicky has been trying to sort out college
for next year, and she's applying for another student loan so
I hope all that works out for her. She got an email off Jacob
yesterday, and apparently it was not a nice one so I don't
what was up with that, sounded a bit like he still would like
to be seeing her still, and he's off working down near the US
border now for a while. I think at some level inside of me
there is still a little hurt from when Nicky was secretive and
all back in May, well there's certainly a lot of blanks or gaps
in what actually was going on, but I have to ask myself do I
really want to know the answers right now? But then there's
the other side of it, which is if Nicky still feels like she has
to keep some stuff hidden, will that cause a gap between us
or something? Not quite sure if it's okay to ask or maybe I
should ask if it's okay to ask? And then on the other side,
if the answers remain only half answered in my head, will
that be more damaging than actually knowing? I think I
am thinking too much here and I'm over tired, not a healthy
mix for me. But it's all because I love Nicky so much and
the last thing I want to do is fuck everything up by asking
or not by asking....

Mon 8th Aug

 Well seems that days are just flying by again, work, study,
last night was a nice chat with Nicky, she had a good trip

out on the lake with her dad and with her aunt. When she was telling me about it, I was finding it hard because I want so much just to be there with her. And so I have a choice here to whether just to go for it now because I mean I could just skip my next assignment, do the last one and then just disappear. Although a big part of me wants that right now I think and Nicky and I will still need some time to test things out, and well this weekend coming, on my road trip, I guess I want to just go mad a little but I also got a lot of stuff to think about, a lot of things to consider. So I will take what time is needed to think through everything, and yes it is true what Nicky said to me, that it does not matter when I do this because we both just know it's going to happen, so it's all good.

I think some of the stuff I was thinking on Saturday is sorted in my head; I think most of it was because I was just tired. I think I need a nice walk tomorrow night because I am not giving my brain enough time to breathe and relax, so yeah, got to get that sorted out too. Oh the stuff Nicky posted still isn't here and that totally sucks, because it would be really cool to get that, really would but its taking too long so it probably ended up getting sent back to Nicky which majorly sucks big time. Anyways, everything else is cool, oh and I found out Nicky levelled a restaurant as a kid, similar to what I done on the forklift at work except she only done a lot more damage. At least no one was hurt, though they never did let me back on the forklift haha. Anyways got to go....

Wed 10th Aug

I've just had a very weird night, I had been cleaning up the house and then I sat down to have a play on my guitar but something real weird happened. I started playing a new song and words came flooding into my head, but I had a very bad freaky feeling and the words were of stuff I dare not speak of. It freaked me right out so I went out for a walk to calm down down but nothing is working. Anyways I don't think I want to talk about that stuff anymore.

The last couple of days at work I have mentioned to a couple of people about me thing of going to Canada, and they were all cool about it, the smile on my face seems to get bigger every day. Nicky has not been herself, well ok she is always herself, but she just seems very stressed out or something, I don't know.

I feel a change in the air once again, and I have felt this before so I got to watch out for those I care about. I miss Nicky a lot, and I love her so much, I think about her all the time. I rang the Canadian embassy today and found out bits and pieces. I think for me to find a job in Canada the best route to go through is sponsorship, so it would take some involvement by Nicky if she is willing to do that for me. Well time will tell, I have a lot of thinking to do for sure, and I'm going to put it all in here, cause this journal is not just about me and Nicky, it's also about our journey till we are together, which may not be too long from now. I'm quite tired tonight, I got to catch up on my sleep before my road trip on Saturday, so I'll probably grab a good night on Friday hopefully, though there's a lot of stuff to get ready too, which I probably should have got done tonight, anyways last night I drew on myself *Rich loves Nicky* on my chest in black and red, and it isn't coming off too good, but anyways, with the markers just sitting here it's just too tempting.

My phone got cut off which is a major pain, though I don't mind really because I couldn't call Nicky anyways, but maybe it's good timing anyways, I might not get it put back on! Got to go....

Mon 15th Aug

Well wow a crazy weekend, I headed off on my road trip early on Saturday morning, after talking for a while with Nicky on Friday evening on the internet and for the first time on the phone since back in June, though bear in mind neither of us have a phone right now. But yea it was cool to hear her voice again, was a little low volume and all but was brilliant to hear that voice I love so much. Well I didn't do as much thinking on my road trip as I would have liked to have done. There are some pretty big decisions here I have to make.

There is something different in Nicky, almost like she is awakening, and she is challenging things she knows and she wants to leave out of her life. Well so my mind isn't sure how or when to make everything happen, but I am sure that I want to go for this. I sleep every night now with two photos in my hand, one of Nicky, one of Ria, and most days I wake to find neither of them here and I know that for me to carry on like this will not be good love for me comes before career and study, and well I suppose my priorities are not right here at the minute and I got to work hard towards those dreams. If only I could move and take Ria with me, it would be simple, but life is never simple, I don't want to make Nicky feel guilty for taking me away from Ria, but it is my choice, and no I never want to spend any days without Ria, but that can never be a reality for me. However being with my sweetheart Nicky, I can wake up to see someone who cares for me as I care for her. So I am thinking, for me to spend a month over there to see how things are, to maybe secure a job offer for a visa application, to see how much I miss Ria. I suppose that me moving to Canada is not the only option for me and Nicky but maybe the only one for now. I still feel inside that I am very different to how my family see me, and maybe the time has come to show the real me, I am over with Stephen and Sarah on Wednesday for dinner, we shall see what happens.

I am weighing up different options for me and I hope I choose right, this is not easy for me, this is hard. I see Ria four days a month, every other day I live this life alone, it's not fair for me, and it's not fair for Ria. Circumstances force me to be a dad in a way that I do not like and I cannot change that, but whatever I decide here; I know for sure that I love Nicky and Ria so much.

Thurs 18th Aug

Conversation continues about getting a visa and Nicky's mum is helping out a lot. Information, that's what we need right now, I am getting really excited about it all, and it's been about six weeks since me and Nicky sorted things out, but to me it feels like we were never apart. Last night was no conversation of depth, but we just chilled out and looked at each other, I told her I loved her which I do with all my heart, I had had a gruelling evening with my brother, but Nicky had me smiling the instant I seen here. Love conquers everything I guess, it certainly conquers me.

The previous night was very wow, the biggest smiles, I think we just smiled constantly for hours, it was very very cool. Also last night was cool when Nicky went over to get comfy on the bed; I teased her a little bit last night but its all good. I can't even sleep at night time now unless Nicky's picture is in my hand, under the pillow with me groping the pillow pretty hard. It's going to be a crazy day tomorrow, crazy at work, have to pick family up from the airport too, at 1am, pick Ria up real early Saturday morning too, have to clean up the house, wow it's going to be very busy.

I don't think I want to go down to Stephen's for a while, I felt very much like they were feeling sorry for me or something, and weren't too interested in the good things going on in my life right now, but hey, I knew it would be like that before I went down there, family !!??!! I wish Nicky was here right now; I miss her and love her, the love of my life.

Mon 22nd Aug

Well what a crazy weekend that was, no sleep on Friday night because had to wait for the plane to arrive in which got delayed, then Ria and I had a cool weekend just doing stuff like going to the park or dancing up in my room. Caught up with Nicky last night, so she was talking to me about all these blokes trying to get with her while she was out and how they all got turned done which is nice to hear. We chatted for a while bout everything like just having a laugh, about marriage, about kids, about me living there.

Well I got to start moving with my plans, got lots to do and organise. Still a little paranoid about telling Nicky dates though, I think I will tell her like a few days before I leave, or maybe the day I'm leaving? We shall see how that one works out, but yea, all speed ahead for this, I have told my brother now about me planning to go get my hands on a visa, he didn't have much to say really, but still have to chat to my mum about it, I will tell Ann closer to the time, when everything is organised. I am a little bit nervous, but I have to follow my heart, but my heart is taking me to Canada, I have been looking for the little signs and all, but I got the feeling the other day, it's the one where I just know it's the right path to take, so I got to do it. I love Nicky so much, and I know not many friends or family understand all this, but that doesn't really bother me what they think anyways, I make up my mind independent of others, and then they choose to support or not to as the case maybe.

So Nicky blew me away a little bit last night by stuff she was saying like how she will love how I snore because she will know I am just there with her. I miss Nicky a lot, especially when I am lying in bed on when I just wake up. I don't believe that our relationship will be instant bliss from the moment I walk into her house, but I know that we will work it all out, and it's going to be pretty amazing. I do feel like the luckiest man alive, I think the world of Nicky, she is so smart, I love her personality, sense of humour, taste in music and films, and wow she's amazingly gorgeous, she's like the woman of my dreams, and then to know on top of all that about how we met, and the odds of it, wow it just blows me away, it's fantastic!

I know I will love Gavin and Lauren, I mean I am great with kids, so that will be cool, I mean they are the most important thing in Nicky's life, I know this move is a pretty big culture adjustment too, it's going to push my boundaries to the extreme in the sense that, I suppose a life her in Ireland is very different to a life in Canada. I trust that I will cope, I am quite adjustable, and besides the Irish are loved everywhere on this planet, never quite understood why that is, it's just that way I guess. But I mean all that really matters is that I really love Nicky with all my heart, and wow just any thought of being there with her just blows me away.

I got to go sort out credit card thing so I can purchase the plane tickets, I am going to book returns flights to Montreal or Toronto but only on way from there which will save a few bob. Wow thinking of sitting on the plane, wow wow wow.

Tues 23rd Aug

Nicky didn't have the best of days yesterday, she was all stressed out like completely stressed and Lisa had come over so we didn't get a chance to talk for too long but that's ok, I love her, and miss her too. I was a bit panicking last night because I can't have Ria this coming weekend as I would have liked, so I have no plans, two days doing nothing, I know I will go insane. Maybe I should head into town or something; I am actually dreading the weekend, how shit is that! I suppose it's because I can't spend it with Ria or Nicky, so I am just sat there thinking about being with them and I go crazy.

I am a slight bit worried about Rachel and Mark too as I have not heard from either of them in a while, though they could have gone off on holidays for a couple of weeks, but Mark is due his results back soon, so I hope it's good news and bad because it will tear them up if he has leukaemia, Mark is a sound chap, looks after Rachel and all. Well I read a nice email Nicky had sent me, just saying some nice things, making me smile again. It's all so cool, just everything is super cool, I love that I have found someone as amazing as Nicky, well I know I am very much head over heels in love.

Well I rang about my credit card and that didn't work out as I had planned because I had missed that payment back in June, but I will pay my way as far as Toronto or Montreal first, and then later book the internal flights, it's just going to be a little more complex that's all. I wonder should I ring the travel agent or just call in on Saturday to them before I pay, got to sort out this financial thing on paper, see how it's going to work, I have to ring the phone company too and get that sorted, so I best do up a list of everything I have to do cause I have to get moving on this pretty fast to make sure it all fits together.

I was downloading heaps of music again last night, which is good, maybe I'll have to buy one of them portable drives so I can bring it all with me. I am bringing my guitar of course. I hope it doesn't get lost in transit or damaged! They don't normally let me take it onto the plane as hand luggage, so got to think about that too. It feels like there is just one final piece to the puzzle and that's in the stuff Nicky has posted to me? So hopefully that will arrive this week! It's all good, well got to go for now....

Wed 24th Aug

Well I sat down with my mum last night and told her about me heading off to Canada to be with Nicky. It went ok, she had a lot of questions to ask and all, but I think she is definitely more down to earth and more realistic than Stephen or my dad; I also put my stuff up for sale, my car and a few other things.

Nicky and I talked last night a little about how we can feel how each other are feeling, like how on Monday I knew how she was having a bad day before she told me, or how last night, I was missing her so much, and she could feel it, or just how sometimes we just meet online as if we knew each other would be there like the time one Friday I signed in as I was heading out the door and so did she right at the same time. Well it's pretty cool, and there's no way anyone could explain how it works, but yeah it's awesome that we can do that.

I learn new bits and pieces about Nicky nearly every day and I love it! I love her. Em looks like the weekend I am heading over there is Halloween weekend which will be extra cool, extra extra fireworks, I think I will buy one of those big Irish hats, just for a laugh then everyone will know this Irishman is in town. I think now about having two months off work or so, and that will be cool, but to spend those two months with Nicky, that will be wow, awesome, I will have to occupy myself while she is at work or college, maybe read through her psychology books, or write more songs on the guitar. I know that if I find black market job or some means of staying, I will stay for an extended period of time, though if I have to return in January, so be it, I will head back for the summer! Wow I got to spend a summer over there.

Mon 29th Aug

Wow what a crazy time I've had over the last few days. Well had a row with Rachel on Thursday because she flipped when I told her I was heading to Canada. Although at the time it just left me stressed, she really did challenge me to ask if this is the right thing for me to do. But the funny thing with that is, the more I think about any doubts, the more convinced I am to go.

Friday night was then a little bit crazy because I was speaking to Nicky when I got in from work and she was supposed to say hi before she went out, and was going to be back in time to chat to me, but kind of let me down. So I lay in bed on Friday night wondering if she was ok and all that, sort of brought me back to April when it used to happen a lot, where she'd say she'd meet me and never be there, so it sucked to have all that back in my head, I found it a little hard to sleep, but it turned out that she had got delayed and we missed each other by about half an hour, still didn't say about how she didn't say bye before she went, anyways.

So I went into town into the travel agents, to change the details for the flights, so I got the dates I wanted, and a much more direct flight at no extra cost which is cool. I have to get together the balance owed by the 15th of September. So Saturday night was a little celebration, I got totally pissed and we had a laugh chatting to each other. Also I ended up asking Nicky to marry me and she said yes, which is cool, though maybe I should have waited to do it in person eh? But yea I know I want to marry Nicky, it would be super cool.

All weekend we just kept chatting at night and during the day, and last night when Gavin and Lauren came home Nicky came online for a smoke, and the kids were saying hi and asking a few questions, like when am I coming, and some other stuff too, of course every time I say hi to them, I ask them to give Nicky a hug from me. Later in the night Lauren came past and waved, she does that every now and again. Nicky and I didn't speak for too long though last night, we were both pretty burnt out, but I think we were both maybe feeling a little bit talked out, that at that moment, we just needed to cuddle or watch a movie, and well we can't do that over the internet, just need to be there for all that.

Tues 30th Aug

Last night was cool, we were up chatting till about four in the morning, and we were just chatting as normal. I kind of went on about how great I think Nicky is. She talked a little about how her mind works in the sense that she seems to put other people's needs ahead of her own, and how she goes all quiet when something is up which is like I am, or definitely how I used to be. Well Nicky totally distressed me last night, because of my friend doing stupid stuff, my head was wrecked but as soon as I seen Nicky it was instant smiles, and I know when she had a bad day that I do the same for her. So it's very cool. So we had fun last night too, wow she knows how to tease me, it was awesome.

I know I have changed a lot in the last year. It's strange that I have accomplished everything I set out to do with my head so it's very cool. I woke up today, and I loved life, I love being here still, life is precious in a way I have never understood before. Just so many little thoughts float around in my head about Nicky during the day. I know I miss her a lot, I went for a two hour walk last night, I had to drop into the hospital to pay a bill, but yeah it was a lovely night, and there's nothing like a nice walk to vent my thoughts.

I still have a couple of big issues to get sorted out here. I need to sell my car and I need to tell Ann that I'm going off to Canada, I know she will not react too good to it, but we chose separate life's well over a year ago, and this is my path now. I do not criticize hers, so yeah I need to think about the worst thing she might do or say, well its Ria I worry about.

Nearly There
Chapter9

From: Nicky> nicky@mynl.com
Sent: 07 October
To: Rich> richard@mynl.com
Oh what happened there I was typing and then when I looked up
I really wasn't because it wouldn't type....I am so stoned .....aaaa
aaaaaaaaaaaaaaaaaaaaaaaaaaaaaaaaaaaaaaaaaaaaaaaaaaaaaaaa
aaaaaaaaaaaaaaaaaaaaaaaaaaaaaaaaaaaaaaaaaaaaaaaaaaaaaaaa
aaaaaaaaaaaaaaaaaaaaaaaaaaaaaaaaaaaaaaaaaaaaaaaaaaaaaaaah
God I am stoned....Richard oh Richard I just want to kiss you
forever and ever....just never ever stop....it amazing...the most
amazing feeling ever...I love you....I love you....Richard I just love
you so much....and you know what my favourite part of the day
is...see after we talk on here I just chill out or whatever.....before
I go to sleep and I put my webcam on I just lay here and watch
you sleep....it's awesome...it's so intense....it's amazing and
that's my favourite part of the day...there was more to that but am
so stoned...and I forgot what I was trying to say...I hate that....
but it doesn't matter cause I love you...it is like wow its intense
eh....I wish you were here right now.... I miss you....Richard I love
you....my cat is going crazy but in the living room....anyways...
you are amazing...just the most amazing man ever... I love
you....how do you do that when you just look at me on here and
I blush...that's awesome....I love you Richard....I find myself in
these day dreams eh...of me and you...it is the most wonderful
thing....my heart just melts...I think of me and you just standing
there facing each other...not a bit of clothes on right...then we
move closer and I am just lost in your eyes at this point...my
heart is going so fast...but at the same time I am so calm almost
as if I know this is the moment I have waited for all my life...
and it's just so amazing...there is just so much love and passion

sometimes I just have to take a deep breath just to get out of that zoned wow state eh...but sometimes I wish I could stay in that moment for the rest of my life...just to feel something that intense that you see it happening in your mind and it's the realist thing ever...and you are amazing....the way you touch me...it's like I know it will be different...something I have never known before...I know when you touch me it's going to be..... too much for words........Richard I love you....when I touch you I will never want to stop....promise me Richard that we will never ever stop.... because this feeling is too intense to ever have to live without...I love you Richard....I will never ever stop loving you...I love you no matter what Richard...forever...and then we are touching each other finally to feel what you feel like to ...to feel you inside me....wow that was by far the best trip I have ever known... if you were here right now oh Richard you don't even know... do you know where I just went...Richard you are amazing.... wow....I just seen me and you...and you were just sitting there on the couch watching TV I just got out of the tub and I walk over to you and you said Nicky I love you....I looked into your eyes and said Richard I love you.... nothing was said after that... we made love I just saw what that was...wow....holy shit....wow Richard...I want to marry you...I want to share my whole life with you forever and ever...I felt that...I felt you inside me...it was so passionate and intense ...I felt you holding my hips while I was on top of you...and we were just looking into each other's eyes... it's just heaven...I feel your hands move up touching my breasts it's the warmest touch I have ever known...you kiss me....wow... Richard... my god....then you are licking my nipples and we are just moving so slow I can feel you go in and out me...it's so amazing....making love to you will be amazing...anyways that's all I felt/seen...and now I am back...what's up...wow I miss you....I need a smoke....wow you are amazing....Richard .....Richard....... Richard..... Richard.... wow....I love you.....I never want to ever stop feeling that incredible most wonderful feeling ever....Richard I want you so much right now....well I should go here...or maybe

I will have a smoke I still never had a smoke since I had that joint after Lauren was asleep...wow Richard oh my god....I felt that... what a trip that was...wow wow wow wow wow wow wow....it was intense....when we are finally together...oh Richard....soon... soon I will be in your arms...I want to be there forever...I want to be yours forever and ever...I want to give you my whole heart, mind, body, and soul....Richard I love you so much ...talk to you soon... mwah infinity...miss you....I need something to eat and maybe a movie not sure yet...wow I miss you....I love you so much...alright good night Richard meet you in our dreams...just heaven...I love you so much, peace.

From: Rich> richard@mynl.com
Sent: 11 October
To: Nicky@mynl.com
Hiya Nicky,

I just wanted to say good morning, I love you so much, and best of luck today with your test, you will do great!!! I miss you and look forward to talking with you later.....I hope you and the kids have a good day.....it's one day closer again to holding you in my arms.... I seen you on webcam this morning.....there was no drool but you looked amazing and I wanted to kiss you and climb in bed beside you.....and then maybe kiss you some more.... mwah mwah... I wanted to talk more here but I got to go for now because I'm at work sneaking in a cheeky email while the bosses aren't looking....one came in the room already....I miss you, I love you so much

hugs and kisses infinity
xoxoxoxoxooxoxoxoxoxoxoxoxoxooxxoxo
Rich

From: Nicky> nicky@mynl.com
Sent: 13 October
To: Rich> richard@mynl.com
Hey so what's up?...I just witnessed the most amazing cover up of all times by a band I love...and I am so stoned but you know I wouldn't have realized what it fucking meant unless I was....

fucking awesome performance...like I said you have to be damn smart to play stupid....Ok I want you see this too so go to the guide on the media player...oh my God it was awesome...I even wanted post something on a site of theirs afterwards because holy fuck.....just well done.... but for some reason it kept on coming up as error when I wanted to type??? I will let you figure that one out mwah...go to the US version of the media player watch the adverts go across the top of the screen and where it says watch the live performance of *Green Day's American idiot* in L.A.....anyways just watch it if you can see what I see out of that performance its crazy....ok here's how I see it well you know the only way they were ever going to be able to perform it was to be approved by *Mr. Bush* himself right...so they get up and do their thing right...but half way through Billy calls 100hundred audience members to come down but doesn't say why...and you can picture Bush freaking out and calling LA... so Billy finally argues with the guards or whatever to let them come down...now this is a live broadcast which means from my knowledge in cinema that it can't be stopped they can't edit it that's given right....and of course million of dollars in shares would be at risk by people who bought the air time including the American government... and all that jazz so you would have to pull a lot of shit off to get them to stop airing it ....so anyways he tells them to come down....and you know why they are doing this right....so that they may have their freedom of speech without any strings attached to Bush...because he could destroy a musical career I will get back to that in a second.... this is amazing...the guys are the smartest people ever....I am truly wowed here....ok so by having 100 witnesses or people that agree with your opinions clears you from what you are really saying....in this case....see they had to do that because they would never have been able to get away with it if they didn't.... and he makes sounds in the microphone and get the audience to repeat...checking to see if the sound is just right...because you know the seating had been done long before they performed just

123

so they would not cause a fuss to the American public...God this awesome....I feel like smoking another here...wow...so anyways then he gets them to sing along with him...and they do loud and clear and just at that very moment Billy turns to the camera and smiles like in your face right...then so do they others...as if to say way ahead of yea right.....then after I watch the video and this is where it gets a bit fucked and I realize all about how it all works in reality eh....the statement made by the media player to grab the American audiences attention reads...Billy Joe calls for more people to come down to the floor for his anthem...Los Angeles loves to hear its name...because Billy kept saying it right...but the media down plays that and say it like the LA'ers are where Hollywood loves to hear it name...you think famous and all that jazz...so this way the media carries the message to the viewer that ...oh never mind I am burning out and hits is sounding ridiculous.....it is awesome though...and the people that sponsor the posted question was *Sony*...that way the US and China would profit off it because so many people would want to check out this performance ...fuck just makes me think by watching it did I really get the message or was it I was tricked into making more money for the US and China to build more bombs really... so in a way what I seen was Green Day gets their message across but only to people of this generation...stoned...or crazy to the "general public or Bush generation"

Funny why they never wanted weed ever to be legalized.... anyways so Green Day gets their message across and does it amazingly without being held accountable by the US government...the US government in turn uses the media to down play events being aired on TV screens around the world so we take the side of the government and good American values... Democracy as some would like to call it....so the rest of the message seen after playing this states....Los Angeles loves to hear its name called by Billy Joe....who wouldn't?....making the audience see it as yea great band...but as like oh yea whatever right.....so in a way they did get their message across but...in the process they are probably going to be ruined by the media... and in turn all this media coverage puts big bucks in the hands of the idiots themselves...I love it in the part of the song when he says that's enough fuck you...I have played that so many times before and... holy fuck... that song means everything I am talking about...but in the end no one believes it because they are not allowed to hear it as it is meant because the message is always misconstrued by the media who is played by the government... fuck it's a fucked up cycle isn't.....it's just funny how the world really works eh...anyways...this is what I mean Richard...I love you...I mean if I would have watched that not stoned I would have never understood on this level...you have to watch it.... life freaks me out sometimes...trippy as hell....anyways check it out let me know what you think because I will be tripping out over this till I see it again not so high myself...and I tell you when I repeat doing things I did when was high I can't remember sometimes but sometimes I do and its pretty trippy too...but it just makes sense...it's amazing...now I know you would never think I was off for saying all this...but really if you would have smoked that and just seen what I seen you would know what I am taking about completely... and it's pretty fucked up... funny how society labels people though... the exact part the media is aiming at...with baby boomers and all the ones that still believe and worship the good old American values and such.... fuck it would even appeal those in that age group that believe in the American dream...come to America...is all that said so we can have more money pumped into the economy of the US to buy more "weapons of mass destruction" because God knows we all know who is holding that wild card...so in a sense *Green Day* is understood by the American audience and maybe even agreed with totally but it just so happens to be the wrong American audience...the one that understands news coverage... followers of the media or the followers of Bush....or sorry good old American values. Democracy...funny...picture the arms.... saying that with a hat and a piece or grass hanging out of my mouth...

fucking red neck.... "God bless those good old American values...
the US wants you" poster child....too funny eh...anyways Richard
I know all of what I said probably sounds a bit crazy but what's
normal eh...think about it...are people who are labelled crazy
...really crazy ...or are they just not following the norm...or values
of a society....hmmmm....I love you Richard I hope you have a
great day I know it's not my typical stoner note here but I had
one of the most awesome highs and seen some "crazy" shit so I
can't complain....I miss you I love you so much Richard....sweet
dreams I am going to meet you there and say all things I wanted
to say to you about me and you....and how much I am in love
with you and that I want to be yours and you to be mine forever
and ever...to be married have more children together...to just
grow old together and to see you again after that...forever and
ever infinity...15days eh....wow...I can't tell you the excitement I
feel it's amazing...to finally be together after such a long wait...
because I believe it's been a lifetime since we parted...mwah you
are the one and you are amazing...I love you Richard...talk to you
soon goodnight, mwah infinity, peace.
From: Rich> richard@mynl.com
Sent: 19 October
To: Nicky> nicky@mynl.com
Hiya babe.....mwah
Well its morning again.....another day of work and another day
closer to when I can hold you in my arms......today is going to
be a mind tiring day because there's just so much paperwork
to get sorted out here at work....I will be gone insane by the
end of the day....today is the last day I have to wear this damn
uniform!! tomorrow I can wear what I like.....God I do hate this
uniform thing...it reminds me of when I went to high school.....I
detest uniforms.....well ok I detest wearing uniforms I should
say...because well if you were wearing a uniform for me that's
a different story ;)....so my mum was saying that probably her
and my dad will take me to the airport next week.....I mean
Stephen did offer that day way back but he is going away that

weekend with his girlfriend so he can't drive me out there.....
it's all good.... I can't wait.....I wish it was tomorrow....wow I love
you so much Nicky....I want to kiss you and never stop.....I love
yousoooooooooooooooooo much....I hope you have an awesome
day just to chill....you deserve that after your days and days of
study.....I miss you Nicky.....I love you talk to you later...hugs
and kisses infinity xooxoxxooxxooxoxxooxoxxoxooxxoxoxoxox-
oxooxxooxoxxooxoxox
P.S.. Which coffees are yea on? First one?

From: Nicky> nicky@mynl.com
Sent: 19 October
To: Rich> richard@mynl.com
Hey mwah I love you too yea it is my first one...and yea that's
cool that your parents will be driving you there...I can't wait
either...it's going to be awesome Richard...so you had to wear
a uniform in high school?...I didn't know that...is it like that over
there everywhere....here we wear whatever we like to school...
its more relaxed I suppose...anyways it's all good...Richard I love
you so much I didn't wake up till 8.15..I guess I missed you when
you were on eh...and then I got back from taking Lauren over to
school and I missed you again...but you know what I love you all
the same...I hope work doesn't end up getting the better of you...
you will get through it, its only a couple more days then you can
chillax some eh...well I am thinking about...missing you too...but
still smiling because you are amazing...and I love you with all my
heart and soul...talk to you soon, mwah infinity, Nicky, peace.
From: Rich> richard@mynl.com
Sent: 20 October
To: Nicky> nicky@mynl.com
Hiya hiya....
I miss you so much these days....and well I just wanted to that
I'm sorry that the next couple of days we won't get much chance
to talk because of my long hours at work tomorrow and because
of my night out on Saturday to have goodbye drinks with my

mates....I know I am going to miss you like crazy....and I wish
you were here to come out with me on Saturday night.....it's my
last Saturday night without being there with you and I will love it
when we head out to party..........I love you so much with all my
heart and soul.....but I will leave my webcam on for you tomorrow
night when I get in for sure....I will say hi too if you are online but
it would have to be a short hi unfortunately......I have that horrible
feeling to face tomorrow at work when I arrive there. Knowing
at 9a.m tomorrow that in the following 32 hours I will be working
24 hours!! (And then going straight from there to the pub) crazy
eh....but I will still be smiling because right at the same time at 9
am tomorrow I can say to myself...this time next week my plane
leaves Ireland.....I love you so so much missing yea like crazy
hugs and kisses infinity
oxoxoxxoxoxoxoxoxooxoxoxo
From: Nicky> nicky@mynl.com
Sent: 21 October
To: Rich> richard@mynl.com
Hey what's up? Alright well I didn't get high tonight...instead I
decided to finish painting the kitchen I know I am insane...but
hopefully it's only temporary...but hey what's insane...or what is
normal eh???....I miss you all the time Richard I really do...but
when I miss you I am never sad because I know that you love
me...I feel that you do ...and that feeling alone makes me smile
all the same....I love you so much...and Richard I understand that
you will be gone the next couple of days and I will miss you but...I
know you got to work and God damn you are going to need to
go out and party it up after all that jazz eh...who wouldn't...I will
busy all the same...so it's all good really...listen all I want is for
you to go and have a great time...just go crazy...you deserve it...
mwah....and our time is coming soon...so don't be worrying about
us missing each other so much because we will be together very
soon...it is going to be awesome eh...when I sit and think about
kissing you for the first time...super intense ...Richard I love
you...I love you...you are amazing ...I would write more but I am

just so tired now....I hope you have a great day tomorrow and hey you are almost finished so it's not so bad you will get through it.. Mwah ...I hope you are having a great sleep and some amazing dreams... I am going to go and meet you there now...talk to you soon mwah infinity...I love you Richard, peace.
From: Nicky> nicky@mynl.com
Sent: 21 October
To: Rich> richard@mynl.com
You are amazing...I am so totally tired...but probably not as tired as you eh...well it will be finished...then you get rest some...with me...mwah...and well maybe not so much rest oh I wish I could kiss you now....wow Richard I love you...I love you so much...I can't till you are here ...I miss you so much...awesome....I love you...mwah...Ok I'm getting so crazy munchies here so ...I will be here if you come on later...if you don't I love you all the same forever and ever infinity...we are so grade 8 eh...but you know it's the best I have ever felt my entire life...true story and everything...mwah infinity forever and ever...I miss you...I love you Richard...talk to you soon
Nicky, peace.
From: Rich> richard@mynl.com
Sent: 24 October
To: Nicky> nicky@mynl.com
Hiya Nicola.....
I love you so much and I hope you day is going well there.... MWAH....well I was in work till like 2 o'clock until I was able to escape out the door...I done some pranks on people but I'll tell you about them later.....and so I have my suitcase sitting here in my room now....and I am starting to stack up my clothes on the floor ready to go.....I got some of my money changed today.... wow your money looks weird lol!!!!......well I know we will get a chance to chat later....I miss yea.....I love you so much....talk to you later
hugs and kisses infinity
Rich

xooxoxoxoxxooxoxoxooxoxooxoxoxoxoxoo
From: Nicky> nicky@mynl.com
Sent: 25 October
To: Rich> richard@mynl.com
Hey what's up? I love you Richard...stoned....but I love you
Richard....I just love you...it's amazing...I miss you...it's like so
intense...I love you....wow I love you....I am freezing now...I love
you I love you I love you I love you I love you I love you I love you
I love you wow I love you I love you I love you I love you I love
you I love you I love you I love ...fuck..My bad I fucked it up...oh
I suck. I suck completely...yes I promise completely. Forever and
ever and ever infinity...I suck....I miss you so much....Richard...
you are amazing...ok wait I had something to tell you....oh wait its
gone...be right back I need to have a smoke....what am I doing...
oh yea Richard I had to tell you something....oh I love this song
when I am high...*Wish You Were Here* by *Pink Floyd*...
awesome ......I love you Richard....you make me so happy. You
are my happy place...I just know it....I know it my heart and in
my mind and soon I will know it with my body...I will know your
touch and will forever want for your touch...when I close my
eyes I can feel it....it's so warm and loving and passionate and
gentle...I so just felt that...amazing...holy amazing...Richard I
love you....I am so thirsty...and anyway see I needed to tell you
something...I needed to tell you that I love you with all my heart
and soul....forever and ever infinity...but I can't stop feeling this
highly anxious feeling....it's like when I think about meeting you
and I am so happy and excited...but for reason sad almost....
maybe it's not sad...I don't what it is I never felt that before....but
yea so I am nervous a little...a little...ok maybe more than that but
anyways...I just love you so much and I just know that we will be
forever...but why do I feel that too....it's like I think about it I see it
I can see meeting you and it's amazing...maybe it's the fact that
it is so amazing...that I feel sad....maybe I feel sad or whatever it
is because if I ever lost that feeling I would...there it is its like this
incredible sadness....but that still doesn't explain why I feel like

130

this eh.......I don't know...I don't know that comes from...I never felt this way before....I really love you Richard...anyway the point of this is just to say I love you...and I miss you...and I hope you have a great day tomorrow...I need to get something to eat... and a drink I am so thirsty....this is a good one when you are burning out...whole lot of love by led zeppelin it's like this craziest awesomest song...every time I hear it. Ever since the first time I heard and got high I just want sex....but its more than that...its oh I can't explain it...it's amazing... a must try when high tune... mwah ok I love you Richard got to go for now...I miss you sweet dreams I will meet you there in a sec...Oh my God I can't stop yawning...just burnt right out here....I love you Richard mwah, Nicky, peace.

Journal Part Three
Chapter 10

Wed 31st Aug

Well it's the last day of August and a very busy month lies ahead of me now, but it is all the better for that, because things will go by faster. I have Ria on Friday night so I'm looking forward to seeing her; we always have such a good laugh together. Things are not great between Ann and I, in the sense that I keep asking to see Ria or talk to her and well she doesn't like changing her plans so much so that Ria can see her dad. I'm still not sure how she's going to react to me telling her I'm heading off to Canada, of course her opinions don't influence me in a anyway, but I'm a little scared she might use Ria as ammunition to threaten me or something or she could be cool about it all. I suppose I just don't know for sure, but I will find out in a while. I want to take a nice photo of me and Ria and give it to Ria to keep in her room because I would like her to have a photo there, well she loves looking at photos anyways.

Nicky and I had problems last night because messenger wasn't working at all, it was crazy, so eventually we got it working. It was just a nice night, I was all chilled out and everything, I went to bed with a big smile on my face, but I just missed her so much I lay there. We talked about having kids, we talked about what we'd like to do when I arrive and the places she wants to show me, and we talked about Gavin and Lauren and about their schooling. I was saying hi to Gavin for a bit last night before he went to bed, he had been following Nicky around because Lauren was not there, but anyways it was cool, I think me and the kids will get on great, and me and Nicky will get on awesomely.

Thurs 1st Sept

Well what another fantastic night me and Nicky had last night. I think I got to bed after three in the morning, so I was a little tired here this morning when I woke, but wow, I mean last night I smiled so much that my jaw was sore, and it was great to be able to de stress Nicky, as David was driving her mad again. Well I have better ways to de-stress her, but I can only do so much from this side of that Atlantic. Well September is finally here, I will be in Canada next month, and I'm so excited about that, I mean I might seem a little crazy to others but I just know how I feel for Nicky and this is something I have to do, I can't believe how lucky I am to have found someone so special, and so wonderful, I am the happiest man alive.

Mon 5th September

Wow what a fantastic thing that happened to me this morning I woke to find a web cam invite from Nicky, I had left mine on all night for her, I sat there and just such a wealth of strong emotion came over me, there really is no words to explain how I felt right at that moment, it was just so amazing. We chatted till after three last night, it was a cool chat, and we just gel so well on many things. We both upgraded our messenger programs, apparently you can make calls on it, so we are going to try that tonight, it will be so cool it that works, I mean it claims to be as good as phone conversations, and well both me and Nicky are without phones right now so it would be great to be able to talk, I miss her voice, we used to chat for endless hours on the phone, and I think we both miss that a lot, I guess I miss Nicky in lots of different ways, like when I am in bed, I miss that she is not there to cuddle with, when I wake or come home from work I miss that she is not there, I love Nicky so much, I can feel it everywhere inside me, My heart, my soul.

I told Ann on Friday about me heading off to Canada, she reacted very different to what I thought she would but in a positive way although she had more to say about it yesterday when I dropped Ria off home. Ann also informed me that she is moving away with her new boyfriend. She has other things to say like how she won't want me collecting Ria from the house or even the estate because Ria might get jeered over it, she also made it clear that when her and her boyfriend Conor have more kids that the other kid will feel left out when Ria is collected, in fact, it seemed like she was trying to make it seem awkward for me to carry on seeing Ria but at the same time telling me how important it is to keep seeing her and how maybe I should not go away for too long, neither was she keen about me taking Ria for the summer holidays over to Canada, but then said she was understanding how we both have to build new futures for ourselves. Our marriage was only ever one sided when we were together and it seems that custody of my daughter still has to remain on her terms, which means basically four days a month and not allowed to take her out of the country, but maybe in the future for a week at most. All her terms and conditions, I understand that my choices in life mean fuck all to her, as hers do to me, yet I think I will have to fight to see Ria in the future, it seemed very much like she did not want me to see her anymore yet was saying the opposite too. It was a little bit confusing.

Tues 6th Sept

Well we tried the messenger call thing and it worked pretty good, it was great to hear Nicky's voice again, actually it was awesome to hear her, the connection was cutting out part of our conversations but well I didn't mind so much just as long as I could talk to her. Well the days are just ticking by, it's getting closer and closer, I rang *Canamerica* to chase the information on my tickets they were supposed to send me out last week, I have to up my motivation levels here on a few things including my study, I guess I have been just sitting back and enjoying August, and put my feet up but I really need to get moving on stuff now, the sooner the better!

Wed 7th Sept

Nicky didn't have a great day yesterday, David had let her down again, which I suppose surprises no one at this point. It does make me angry to hear the things he calls Nicky. I will just try best to be understanding and supportive to Nicky, as I know how hard it can be. But anyways Nicky then got the stuff I had sent her a few weeks back, perfect timing!! Another co-incidence to add to our list, it's awesome, so the music and letter helped cheer her up a little bit. By the time we said good night last night we were both buzzing off the news that we'll spend our first days together in Halifax, and we talked about what we're going to do, and go see, her dad Ethan is coming to Halifax that weekend, another con-incidence? So it's working out great.

Mon 12th Sept

Yeah so I had a real busy few days just gone by! Big sale at work yesterday but I tell you it was awesome just to go home, chill out, and then call Nicky and have a drink while we chatted on messenger, I was in an awesomely happy mood last night, it was cool, it's great to be happy!

So I have the money ready for buying my tickets on Thursday, and they approved my afternoon off work to go and do it. I read my star signs in the paper today and it was awesome, it mentioned Canada, really awesome, I am going to try and tear it out of the paper so I can keep it, besides I got to tell Nicky about it! I had great fun last night teasing Nicky with my box of *Pringles*, it was awesome, I think about Nicky all the time, there is nothing in my life I have ever believed in so much, that Nicky and I are just meant to be. Sometimes I worry that something might go wrong like me losing my passport or something like that, but I got to trust that it will be ok, and things really do just seem to be coming together in an awesome way! So far so good and forty six days to go, bring it! I am a little nervous because all the new faces I am going to be meeting but one thing is for sure and that that I want to keep contact with all my friends here by email or letter. I found some old letters there the other day, was a bit of a memory trip. I know letting go of friends has always been tough for me and that's why I want to keep contact now with everyone. Oh yes Simon rang on Friday and offered to advertise my car for sale…awesome! Ok got to go back to work now.

Wed 14th Sept

Well there's still no sign of the stuff Nicky posted over to me which sucks big time, well I suppose I might try to see if its sitting down at the post office or something, but after that I think I will have to give up waiting for that because it's just not going to get here, I mean its September, and the stuff was sent a few times, first back in April, so yea I have waited too long. Tomorrow is the big day where I have to go pay for my tickets, I think I would have preferred to get a walk in tonight sometime but I have to work till midnight. I got to say hi to Nicky this morning, but will probably not get the chance to see her later on because I will be wrecked, I will miss her, tomorrow is a massive massive day because of the let down back in May that hurt a lot, this is a big step for the trust in Nicky that has been rebuilding, well got to go head into work now.

Friday 16th Sept

Well I paid the tickets yesterday, made one more slight change to them, and only had to pay an extra twenty quid, but that was because of the changes in tax, but it was some hole I burnt in my pocket yesterday, it was crazy, but worth it.

Ria is not well so I've been asked not to keep her overnight so I'll head down in the morning to see her. I got a chance to say hi to Lauren and Gavin yesterday again, there were in jumping on Nicky's bed, and then we were pulling faces at each other for a little while. I had an amazing dream yesterday and all it was, was a kiss with Nicky, but it was so real, and so intense, wow it was so amazing. Well it's another day gone, it six weeks from today and I can't wait to finally be with Nicky, I love her so much, it's going to be cool, awesome and nice just to be able to hang out with her face and do stuff, have fun, kissing etc, can't wait!

Tues 18th Sept

Busy busy week ahead, but time will go faster! It's my brother's birthday today, so it will be a bit of a family gathering tonight. Nicky last night was real tired, she had a long day, it was great to see her smiling and even blushing, though I have done a lot of smiling too, It was mentioned that she might need time before it settles in that all this is real, you know, once I am there and all. I suppose I will be the same, I have no doubts over how I feel or how me and Nicky will get on together, its I suppose, having a relationship behind those computer screens creates a situation where it's not real, but nothing is face to face so it's not real in that way, know what I mean? So when I am finally there, it might take some time to readjust to being face to face. Yes it's going to be much more awesome than just typing or seeing each other on webcam, that's for sure. I put up in a message the other day to have faith, you need something to believe in, and I believe in us. I can't explain how I am able to drop everything and just leave to be with Nicky, I love her so much, but this is about more than how I feel about Nicky, it's also about my destiny, and about my fulfilling who I am, and who I can be, When I feel Nicky's love in my heart, I find it helps me overtake anything facing me, and I am, and I will continue to talking about our relationship, maybe it's time to start things a new and better way, we are always smiling, I guess two people in love are meant to be this happy!

Wed 21st Sept

I have this feeling, because time is going past so quick, it's like when you know something is approaching and you feel you had loads to do before the time arrives. Well that's what I feel like today. I mean it's a good thing because it motivates me to get on with selling my car, and everything else. I have got two of my job references in now, and I just need the one more, but I'll be asking for that one when I hand in my notice next week. I mean it's great that time is going past so fast because I am looking forward to being with Nicky so much! I love her more and more each day. A big chunk of my worries will be gone when my car is sold, I mean I know I'll sell it, but I suppose the more I get for it the better, I love Nicky so much, I'm not so much missing her today, I'm rather just thinking about her with a happy smile on my face.

Wed 28th Sept

Well a month from today I will be stepping on a plane to Canada. I'm also going to hand in my notice at work today, going to finish around the 21st of October. I went on a long walk last night to think about things. I was a little worried because Nicky had been so upset on Sunday, so I needed to think about that. Also with what that conversation with Ann last week about Ria had knocked me for six thought I seem to have maybe sorted that out now, thanks to some advice from Nicky. We haven't had much chance to talk as much as normal over the last five days, I am missing

Nicky a lot last night she was just real tired, the previous night she was looking over my assignment for me, and the nights before she headed off the watch a movie with her sister upstairs. But I suppose it's all good, absence makes the heart grow fonder, and yes I am missing Nicky loads, the last couple of nights we used the voice conversation thing a bit more, I think I would have liked to be using it all the time now, talking and typing are just not the same! Well one of the things I was thinking about last night was what if things go wrong with my trip, as in delayed flight, or maybe Ethan might get a puncture, I think I needed those thoughts just to calm down, I mean things in life never worked out for me the way I would have planned, and maybe because of my May trip going wrong, I still get worried sometimes. I don't doubt Nicky or our feelings for each other, it's just that, that night back in the summer will always remain a moment which I will look back to and think ouch that really really hurt. But I know my pain was less than what Nicky faced in those months, I love her very very much. Well I got to head into work now. I hope to maybe write some more later too, it's been a crazy few days with weekend work and trying to get the assignment finished and all. I hope Nicky and I get a bit longer to chat tonight, I miss her so much right now.

Thurs 29th Sept

Well we chatted till after three in the morning last night. I think the computer lost the connection or something because both cameras were off when I woke up this morning. I find it very hard some mornings, because well I'd love to be waking up beside Nicky and I miss her then a lot, but if I see her on webcam, even if it's only for a few minutes, I don't miss her so much. It's not so hard when I am heading to bed because I am nearly always talking to her right up to when I crash out in bed, though I do wish she was there, that would be real nice.

Wed 5th Oct

Well I've had quite a few busy days; I have twenty three days left now in the country. My car was sold and gone yesterday, which has been a big worry for me, mainly because I had to try and sell it when it needed a few jobs doing to it. But it's gone now, so I don't need to worry about it anymore. I had Ria on the weekend just gone which was great because I had been missing her a lot, but then when she was here, I found it hard too, because well I know that having her here that it can't just be me and her, there's always other people around, and although Ria loves them all, it's just I'd rather just have that time for me and her, especially now that I am going soon. The reality of it is that I can never be the father I want to be, and I can never be the father that Ria would like me to be, maybe that's the curse of how society is today, I mean maybe there is a balance for those who are lucky eh.

Nicky and I talk a lot more through the voice thing on messenger, sometimes if it cuts out because of reception or whatever but I am loving being able to hear Nicky. I know that I do miss Nicky more and more each day, and we just get on better and better, I mean we would be talking and Nicky would say how she is with something, and it would be the same way I am with something. I know we have a lot in common, in many ways and I know and believe that my weaknesses are helped by strengths, almost as if we are just meant to be as if we were separated at birth and now re joined to be one again, it's the most intense amazing thought ever.

Tues 11th Oct

I seem to write less in the journal lately, I think maybe it's got to do with me being so busy all day getting stuff prepared for when I leave, also Nicky and I talk more by voice, like two or three hours a night. Well Nicky had a couple of tests at college over the next couple of days so we won't get to talk much. Well she has reading and studying to do. I have continued to feel my love growing for her, sometimes it's just intense and I just get lost for words, and I miss Nicky a lot more now, if I go even a day without saying hi, I miss her like crazy, but it's mostly missing her but I would be still smiling. I have thought about a lot of stuff these past few days I knew the weekend just gone was my last weekend that I have to myself before I head off to Canada. I have to pack up stuff like CDs and DVDs and last night I spent the evening clearing out my stuff from Ria's room. Also I've started deleting files off my computer, I have some left to do I got my mp3 player sorted out for the journey too, all this stuff takes time which is making the days go by faster, it's a strange feeling really because it's like the days don't go by fast enough, because I want to be on the plane right now! But also each day does by itself go by very fast, which I suppose is good. I have Ria this weekend, I hope we have a good time together, I'm sure we will, I know I will miss her, but Ann had almost removed her from my life as it is, I would take Ria with me if I could but I can't.

Mon 24th Oct

It's almost two weeks since I've wrote in here but it's definitely feels like I haven't had any spare time in the last few weeks, and so this is the big week, these are the days and nights that will go past so slow. I guess right now I am really excited but at the same time a little nervous, I will be happy when I am there safe and sound. I was working the weekend just gone, I had to take a photo to work with me of Nicky just to keep me going, and even tonight when I was freaking out a little, the words Nicky spoke to me of what will be will be just helped calm me down so much, She makes me smile no matter how I feel inside, and I know this weeks will be on intense week for so many reasons but I know I can make it through.

Tues 25th Oct

Well I am a lot more chillaxed today, maybe I needed that sleep I got last night. Well it was a little worrying last night to learn that hurricane Wilma was travelling up the coast, heading for Nova Scotia, but I reckon it will be okay, it does look very menacing on the web sites, watching it twirl its way north.

So arrangements for the weekend have changed because we won't be spending Saturday night in Halifax but it's all good. I will be happy just to be there safe and sound. Heading out with the family tonight, they get very competitive over bowling, especially Stephen who always seems to need to win. It doesn't look like I will see Ria before I leave, I have spoken to her and all on the phone, but they are moving house today which has just made it hard to get to see her and Ann wouldn't let me.

Halifax and Sydney
Chaper11

Richard walks out of the door to the airport with Nicky. Nicky's dad Ethan pulls up in this big jeep thing; they call them a 'truck' over there in Canada, whereas truck to Richard means something else. It was a huge jeep, metallic silver in colour and it had front and back seats as well as the big open back for carrying things which is so different to anything Richard had ever seen before.

"You can put your stuff in the back there" said Nicky.

"Ok sound" as he lifts his guitar and bags over the sides of the truck and into the back.

Richard climbs into the back seat.

"Hey boy, how are you?" asks Ethan from the driver seat.

"Ah I'm grand, how are you?" he replies.

Richard feels Nicky slipping her hand into his. Her cold skin feels so soft to the touch.

"Ha your fingers are long like mine" he says with a smile.

Their eyes meet and she smiles, she wants to kiss him so bad but her dad is there so she looks down. Richard looks around in the inside of the 'truck', Ethan looks a little bit like his own dad except Ethan is a bit more slender looking and has more hair on his head, but he does have a similar moustache and square shaped jaw which was far from clean shaven.

"We have to stop off at the mall, is that ok?" Nicky says to Richard

"Emma is there buying a few things, maybe we could have a look around, you could get some beers for tonight if you want?" she asks.

"Ok ya cool" he replies.

When they get to the mall Ethan just pulls up as he doesn't want to leave the truck to go in, which suits Richard as all his stuff is in the back. Richard and Nicky get out and have a bit of a stroll around, gripping each other's hand tightly; it had been so long waiting just to do these simple things. They walk around, Richard feels happier than he has done in years, and people walking past them were probably wondering what they are so damn happy about and where could they get some of that happiness!

"Oh hey there's Emma" Nicky says to Richard and pulls him over to introduce him.

"Hey Emma" Nicky says.

"Hey" Emma says.

"This is Richard" Nicky says turning to Richard and smiling up at him.

"Hey Richard" Emma says politely.

"Do you know where dad is?" Emma asks.

"He's parked up out front, we are just going to grab a few beers and we'll meet you there" Nicky says.

Getting back to the truck they head off to the hotel in the centre of Halifax. They drive down into the underground car park. Ethan and Nicky help Richard carry his stuff to the lift and then to the room. Nicky had told Richard that her dad needed to go to Halifax that weekend for a conference but he kind of figured out pretty soon that Ethan wasn't there for a conference, he was there to browse Halifax and also get to see if the Irish man is some sort of freak so he could then protect his daughter. I can imagine their chat now driving up to the airport he probably said 'hey you know if it's not who you think or if you don't like him, run out quick and we'll make a quick getaway eh'. Canadians do that. They say "eh" a lot. If it was my daughter, I would do the exact same thing, and I think any good father would.

The hotel room was huge. Maybe the Canadians like things big just like the Americans. It had a big sitting room with a kitchen attached, and then two bedrooms off from that. Nicky explains to Richard that Ethan has one room and her sister Emma the other and that they would have the pull out sofa. He doesn't mind! To be lying next to what he thought was the most gorgeous girl on the planet, he did not care what they were lying on. In his head though he was thinking it would have made more sense if they had a room instead of Emma, for the privacy, but that's probably exactly why they were on the sofa bed, so that they would not have any privacy, probably another plan arranged by Ethan. Richard wasn't angry with Ethan, sure he was paying for the room and everything! Anyways Ethan had disappeared off somewhere.

"Where do I leave my- -"said Richard.

"Just leave them anywhere I guess" said Nicky.

Nicky goes to the fridge and puts away the beers they had bought into the fridge while Richard puts his bags neatly over by the wall. They stand in the kitchen and they open a beer each.

"You hungry?" asks Nicky.

"Ya I'm starving, I've not had anything proper to eat since I left Ireland! Are we going to go somewhere to eat or- -"

"Well when my dad gets back we'll grab a key and go out eh" she says.

When Ethan returns he has extra keys and he gives one to Nicky so the two love birds head off out. They go walking around Halifax; Nicky had been there loads of times before so she had a few places where she thought she might like to take Richard. She leads him into a place which is a bar combined restaurant place, it looked a bit run down and there was broken peanut shells all over the ground, I think that was something to do with it being Halloween but even still it was strange. The place was a bit run down, when they served Richard up burger and chips, he gobbled it down quicker than he could taste it. They didn't have any alcohol that bared any resemblance to anything on the other side of the Atlantic, so Nicky suggested a beer to him to try that she usually drinks. He wasn't taking in much notice of names of restaurants or which turn on which street or which name of which beer because the only thing he was soaking up was how amazing this beautiful woman was that was sat with him. He felt the luckiest man in the world and couldn't stop smiling.

They left that place and headed to the Irish bar. She had told him about this place before he had even left for Canada; it had been in the plans to go there while they were in Halifax. You must remember that it was her love for all things Irish that ended up with them in this position. Entering the bar they choose a quiet little table by the window, which looked out past the decorative ironwork onto the road. There was a live band in there playing live Irish music. It did not feel like Canada, It felt like Ireland. But Irish pubs are spread so much around the whole globe, it's one of Ireland's great exports, although some of the so called Irish pubs spotted around the Mediterranean aren't exactly places you'd be proud of, this place on the other hand was nice. Richard went to order a round of drinks from the bar which was decorated with all sorts of authentic Irish souvenirs, to his surprise they had a cider there on tap, not an Irish one but an English one, he could settle for that as the next best thing, with alcohol drinks that he knows being so scarce around here, he doesn't know when he would next have one that he likes, as he's not a big fan of beer although he would drink it if there is nothing else. They sit there for a number of hours chatting, drinking laughing smoking, well she smoked, and although he did smoke occasionally he wasn't that night.

"You must be getting tired?" Nicky asks looking at Richard tired face.

"Ya I am a bit though I'm really enjoying it here" he replied.

"Well how about we head back to the room and you can get a bit of sleep or whatever" she says.

Richard's mind wanders off to what the 'whatever' might mean.

"Yea ok then, finish our beers first?" he says.

  Richard did feel that he needed to put his head down to at least rest, it had been a long old day for him as technically he had only left Dublin that morning, and got three flights, first to London, then Newfoundland and finally Halifax. He felt though that he didn't want to sleep, he didn't want to miss one moment of being with Nicky. They get back to the hotel room, and they tip toe around as they are the last ones in and well they didn't want to make too much noise. They stand there; in the dark room with no lights on, looking at each other they kiss passionately. Nicky gently lifts his t-shirt up over his head, and he lift hers top off. He kisses her neck real slow. Nicky undoes his jeans buttons one my one, and they drop to the floor. He unbuttons hers and slowly pulls them down over her legs. He thinks she has purposely wanted to tease him. She is wearing lace knickers, which is his favourite, and she looks so much sexier than she ever did on web cam. They climb into the covers, well just in case anyone walks in, as they don't exactly have a huge amount of privacy there and they didn't want to be caught being busy at it. They carry on kissing; he runs his hand down along her body and into her knickers. He plays with her, immediately she starts moaning with pleasure.

"Shhhhh" he says.

"Oh right, I didn't realise I was - - , it just feels awesome" she says smiling.

They hadn't talked about what they might do that night, but one thing became immediately clear, that they would not be able to do very much for the noise levels would surely wake up their neighbours, and well what a great first impression Richard would be making on her relatives. He pulls her knickers down and off and continues to play with her, teasing her intensely with his hand, he could tell she wanted him really bad as she was turned on by the way he was touching her. She climbs over on top of him. His hands run down her soft back and he holds her against him as she rubs off against him. Even in that darkened room she looks beautiful to him. She leans back and undoes her bra.

"Oh my God" Richard says quietly to himself as he lifts his hand up to caress her breasts. He knew she had a nice bust the theses were DD in size and very voluptuous. She leans back down, kissing his chest, then his stomach and she takes him out of his boxer shorts and puts him in her mouth, he can tell by the way she touches him that she loves to tease just as much as he does. They want each other so much, to make love for the first time, something which they have waited so long for, but with neighbours and thin walls, they stop there; love would have to wait just one more night.

Richard wakes up, his arms are still wrapped tight around Nicky, and just exactly where he had left them when he fell asleep. It will probably take a few nights before he can get used to that one. He enjoys the moment and holds her as close as he can without waking her. It's about twenty minutes before she opens her eyes and they look at each other.

"Good morning gorgeous" Richard says.

"Morning" she replies and smiles and then pulls the covers up over her face leaving just her eyes.

"I'm not really a morning person" she says.

"That's ok babe" he replies.

"Hey how about we go down to Tim's, you know the coffee place I told you about, you like coffee right?" asks Nicky.

"Come on then" and he hops out of bed throwing on his jeans socks and t-shirt. Nicky slowly puts on some clothes too; she puts on a hoody jumper and lifts the hood up over her hair.

"Ok so how do you like your coffee?" Nicky asks as they walk down the hill from the hotel.

"Ah I'd say fairly strong with two sugars and milk" said Richard.

"Ok so you should ask for a double double, first double is for the size and second is for the sugars" Says Nicky.

When they get there it's not open yet. Nicky goes and sits on a nearby step. She keeps ducking and diving with her head, now and again she'll look at Richard, just for a couple of seconds smile and then turn away.

149

"Why won't you look at me?"Richard asks.

"Cause " she says.

Richard sits down beside her on the step.

"Cause what?" he asks.

"Cause I don't want you to see me like this, without my make up on and hair done" she replies.

Richard puts his hand to the side of her face and draws her eyes up to meet his.

"You don't need to hide, you are so beautiful just the way you are, you don't need make up and I love your crazy hair" Richards says and she smiles. For a moment she forgets her insecurities and looks deep into his eyes, and she kisses him. They are interrupted by the noise of the door of the coffee place being unlocked, they are now open. They go in and order a coffee each, well they are both big fans of coffee, and Richard almost lives on the stuff, but that coffee was pretty good, enough to kick a bit of life into any person unlucky enough to have worst hang over combined with lack of sleep. So I guess it will do. It was cheap too. Though everything there is tax, it's like there's the price, there's the tax. Really different to "rip off Ireland" as so much of us Irish have experienced of companies upping prices adding taxes and currency changes all in a hidden way as almost just to rip you off. So they headed off back to the hotel sipping their coffees and walking along slowly.

They strolled into the hotel dining area and Ethan was there reading a coffee and having his breakfast. He was nearly finished by then and Emma had already eaten and gone upstairs to pack. So Richard and Nicky sat there with her dad chatting for a bit and telling him where they had gone the night before and Richard also talked to him about what kind of work he would be looking for. Ethan went off to the hotel room and they followed him not long after. They packed up their stuff and then loaded the 'truck' and got on the road to Sydney which is where Nicky and the others lived, and I guess where Richard lived now too! It's not really a short journey; it takes about four hours to do it by car. Richard didn't mind so much, he was soaking up the views and all of this new country he had never seen before. It seemed to him very much like what he had seen of Newfoundland when he stopped off there. There are just trees, loads and loads of trees. Ok yes of course there are houses and cities in Canada, but on that four hour drive, there was just tree after tree after tree, and it was autumn so all the trees were this wonderful colour of red and orange. It was strange when they crossed the causeway though. Sydney is on Cape Breton and the Cape is joined to the mainland by a causeway, and there are some amazingly beautiful places there in Cape Breton. However it was strange for Richard as he had seen the causeway on road cameras on that web link Nicky had given to him ages ago. He was feeling a little bit nervous about everything, new country, new town, new opportunities, and there were the big things too like meeting Lauren and Gavin for the first time, are they going to get along ok, where will he find a job, where does he start with finding a job, will he get a job when his status in the country is somewhat questionable.

"You ok?" Nicky asks Richard as he had been sitting there quietly.

"Ya I'm ok, just taking in all the scenery" he replies

"Oh hey I forgot to mention to you, the kids are coming back tonight, is that ok?"

"What happened? I thought David - - "

"Yea I know he was supposed to looking after the kids till tomorrow but he said he's got to work tonight, it sucks cause I wanted to spent time with just me and you." Nicky says as she grabs and holds him arm.

"Ah it's alright with me, I'm looking forward to meeting the kids" says Richard.

"You sure?" asks Nicky looking at him

"Ya of course" he says, smiling at her and then returning his gaze out the window. It was Saturday, and well David had taken the kids the day before and usually he would take them for the weekend. The battle with David was an ongoing thing, he would always try to be as awkward as possible, well from what Richard had heard of him and from all the things he had pulled on Nicky since he had known her. In some ways Richard and David were very similar; they were both separated from their ex's and had kids with them. Well Richard had one kid while David had the two. Life for a man separated from his kids is a hard thing to accept, and not many people recognise that fact. Being used to seeing your kid every day, and that being the highlight of your day, to suddenly have that gone from your life, well not totally gone, but gone in part, it's never the same again. Some dads I guess can't deal with that and they decide it's easier emotional wise to disappear off the scene because they cannot deal with the complex emotions that go along with these sorts of circumstances. Other dads fight, they fight hard to see their kids, and they don't accept not being around their kids, they do what it takes through courts and solicitors and settlements to ensure they maintain their relationship with their kids. Richard was neither of these; he was a bit of a mix. He found the complex emotions very hard to cope with, especially the first day he seen Ria's car seat in the back of the car of his ex's new partner. He had however never used Ria as a tool to get at his ex, had always done his best to try and support her and had always given money to Ann to make sure Ria was ok, in fact he paid her eight weeks in advance to make sure he was ahead on payments before he left Ireland, to give him a bit of time to find work and all. David was different though he was the type who makes things as difficult as possible, the type who messes about with money to support their kids. The one who messes about when he is taking the kids for visits and messes the kids about, and from what Richard knew of him he could not understand how any dad could be like that. There's not one day he doesn't wish that Ria could be there with him to share it, he struggled to accept she can't but he still wished it and valued every minute of time he got with her. He was worried too about how David will react with him being there in the house with Nicky and the kids. The rest of the drive was a bit of a blur for Richard, maybe because looking out the window at loads of trees can make it blurry, but also he was thinking about all this stuff, and well he was quiet too around Ethan and Emma as he is usually shy around people he has not met before, but he did try his best to chat to them. They eventually come into the outskirts of Sydney; it's nearly dark at this stage. Sydney is a small town; all the houses are made of wood, which is strange to anyone who has never seen a wooden house in their life. Ethan drives the truck up beside a big grey house, its Nicky's place.

They all get out, well apart from Ethan as he was heading off home. Emma lived in the flat above Nicky. It did used to be one complete house but it had been adapted so that Nicky and Emma could live there separately. The house was owned by Ethan but he let his daughters live there. It was a big house, was sort of the house if you close your eyes and imagine a haunted house on the hill would look like. Nicky helped Richard with his bags to the front porch. It was like a porch he had seen on TV in America and there was some stuff stored there like garden chairs and that, obviously because it was no longer summer. Again there was a "door screen" he's not sure if that's what you call it, it's a see through door that you leave closed to keep insects out if you leave the real door behind it open so that you get some cool air coming in the summer. Richard didn't quite understand it, never seen one before apart from on TV. They go inside through the door; they walk into a hall which extends into the living room, big tall ceilings and big old iron radiators. Nicky gives him the tour. To the immediate right is another small hall and off that are two doors which are the kid's bedrooms. After that, midway along the sitting room is another door to the right, this is Nicky's bedroom and now Richard's too. If you keep walking through an arch into the kitchen diner which was quite small but of a reasonable size, off the kitchen led two ways, ahead to the left was the utility room with a washer and dryer and to the right led a door to the staircase and back garden. Although there was a staircase, at the top of the stairs was Emma's flat and that door was never opened. Nicky leads Richard back into the bedroom.

"I've made some space for you, there's some hanging space there "she says, pointing to the right hand side of the built in wardrobe.

"And you can have this shelf too" pointing at a shelf area above the hanging space.

"I've got to get a few things to do before the kids get home, are you alright to - -"

"Yea, that's perfect, I'll get unpacked" he replies.

"Oh is there somewhere to leave my empty cases and all?" he asks.

"Yea there's space in the cupboard behind the front door, there should be enough space there, if not then we'll find somewhere eh?"

Richard nods his head and lifts a case up onto the bed and unzips it. He hangs up all his clothes in the wardrobe and puts his socks and boxers on the shelf with a few personal items. He leaves his green bag which had all bits and pieces like CDs and DVDs and all his money down on the ground by the end of the bed as well as his guitar. He takes the empty suitcase around to the front door and finds just enough space in the cupboard and has to lean it back against the cupboard door in order to make it fit. 'Hmm unpacked in my new home' he thinks to himself and goes to find Nicky in the kitchen sorting out some clothes.

"I'm all unpacked, what time do you think the kids will be here?"Says Richard

"They'll be here pretty soon, is it ok if we head down to the supermarket? I need to get a few bits" she asks him.

Richard fetches his jacket. It was a bright blue jacket which was windproof and waterproof so well suited to the weather there, well he hopes anyways. They walk down the street to the crossroads and press the pedestrian button; it's on one of the main roads in Sydney so it's not like in Ireland where you just run across when you get the chance. They skip across the road when the walk now light comes on and then across the next road and into the car park of the supermarket. The jacket works so far, Richard didn't feel one bit cold. The first thing he notices about Canadian supermarkets is a lot of the brands and stuff available is so different to Ireland, I mean you still get similar cereals to Ireland but something's are totally different, the butter, the milk and the list goes on. They grab a few bits of what Nicky says they need and Richard carries the bags as they walk back to the house. It's dark out now. Pitch black. The house looks even more haunted in the dark when you walk up to it. It's cool though, he likes it here already. They go inside to the warmth and Richard does his best to help unpack the shopping, considering that he doesn't know his way around the kitchen yet. There's a knock at the door.

Settling In
Chapter12

Nicky goes to the front door as it opens with Lauren and Gavin running in past her. Richard is still stood out in the kitchen by the sink. He is almost scared to move, scared of what David might say to see him in the house, and well nervous about the first meeting with the kids, he didn't want it to be a first meeting with them seeing some big argument between their dad and some new guy they had never seen face to face before. Yes he had said hello to them plenty of times on messenger when he was talking to Nicky, but this is so different. He hears Nicky and David talking by the front door but he can't make out what they are saying. Nicky closes the door and comes in the kitchen and starts unpacking the kid's overnight bags, putting the dirty clothes in the washing machine. Lauren and Gavin walk into the kitchen.

"Hi Richard" Lauren says, breaking the ice.

"Hi Lauren, how are you?" Richard says.

"I'm ok" she says smiling, Gavin is half stood behind her glancing out at him.

"Hey mum, do you know where my homework is?" Lauren asks.

"Mmmm I think it's still in your bag in your room" replies Nicky.

Nicky asks Richard "Hey why don't go sit down and chillax and watch some TV while I go through homework with Lauren?"

Richard smiles and nods his head and goes in and sit down on the sofa and switches on the TV, Gavin follows him in from the kitchen and sits on the other sofa.

"So does this mean I have another sister?" Gavin blurts out.

"Yes of course you do" Richard says.

"When do I get to meet her?" he replies.

He's only five and doesn't understand the huge complexities in such a task.

"Hopefully in the summer holidays" Richard says.

Lauren walks back across the room into the kitchen with some books in her hand. Richard starts flicking between stations now that the questions have stopped.

"So did you have a good time at your dad's?" Richard asks Gavin.

"Yea it was ok, he slept a lot though" he replies.

"Oh ok, so how come he - -"

"I like this, can we watch this?" asks Gavin, interrupting Richard.

"Yea ok, sure I like the Simpsons too...so how come your dad was sleeping?" asks Richard.

"I don't know but he didn't get out of bed for ages and I was bored" Richard smiled imagining kids sat bored in a room and a dad sleeping in the next room not getting up till the afternoon and the kids had nothing to do. Nicky and Lauren join them for a while. They sit and watch TV and then Nicky goes gets them ready for bed and the kids say goodnight to Richard. Nicky spends quite a while in their rooms before re-appearing; obviously kids have a lot of questions to ask her. If felt quite strange. You know those packets of powder and you add milk and make stir it up a bit and then let it settle and then you have dessert. It kind of felt a bit like that to Richard. It was like instant family and that's a very strange thought. Nicky came back in the room and sat next to Richard on the sofa and he puts his arm around her.

"You know Gavin asked me if he has another sister, and when could he get to see her"

"Really what did you say?" asks Nicky

"I said that hopefully she would come over in the summer" he says.

"Richard I love you" she says.

"I love you too Nicky" and Richard leans over and kisses her.

Right there, right at moment, if you were there and stood in the room with them and looked at the clock on the wall you would have seen it stop, as time for them stood still. They could see deep into each other's eyes, into each other's souls, smiling and so happy to finally be together after such a long journey. They get up and head to the bedroom, he grabs her hand and holds her against him and kisses her passionately. She then heads off to the bathroom to brush her teeth. He sits there on the edge of the bed, nervous, happy, and excited. She comes in and he stands up and kisses her slowly, looking into her eyes. He softly lifts her blue top up and over her head. Kissing her again, he moves down her neck, kissing her ever so softly, she can feel his breath from his nose caressing her skin and his lips randomly pressing against her. She lifts his top up over his head, and then runs her hands up his back holding him close, kissing on the lips again; all the nerves have gone removed by an inexpressible desire to be one with the girl he loves. He unhooks her bra and feels her nice warm skin up against his. She undoes his jean buttons, one by one and he hears them drop to the floor so he steps out of them. Then he undoes her jeans and takes them off her. She turns so that her back is facing him, turning her head back and kissing him, His hand wanders down inside the inside of her knickers while his other hand caresses her breasts. She moans as he starts to play with her, getting her nice and turned on, she can feel he's hard and pressing at her through his boxers which were somehow still on. She takes a hold of her knickers and bends over removing them and giving him a great view, this is his favourite position so all this teasing was making him really turned on. "Lie on the bed so I can put my head between your legs" he says to her.

"No, I want you to fuck me right here, right now" Nicky says looking at him through her seductive eyes.

He takes his boxers off, Nicky leans forward a bit reaching down between her own legs she places him in the right place so he pushes slowly until he is inside of her, 'it feels so good' he thinks to himself. Holding her hips as she is leaning over, he pulls her against him and then lets her pull out a bit. She's the perfect height; he grabs her hair with one hand.

"God I love your wild hair" he says to her.

They just keep getting faster and faster, she loves to make noise and doesn't hold anything back. Sweat starts to drip from his forehead; He reaches around with his hand and play with her at the same time. Nicky lets out a scream as she climaxes. Not content to leave it at that, she leads him by the hand out through the bedroom door. "Where are we going now?" Richard asks, as he looks around noticing that there aren't even curtains up over the windows in the sitting room and one can see straight out onto the street. She leads him into the kitchen and leans over the kitchen table. He is still aroused and eases himself back inside of her he can feel the immediate benefits of the table, it means he can go so hard and she can't move anywhere. Nicky lets out a little moan of discomfort so he puts his hands by her hips at the top of her legs as a buffer between her and the table, was also for a bit of grip as his feet were slipping on the floor. Richard gets close to climaxing, so he pulls out quick as he doesn't want the fun to stop here. "What are you doing eh" she asks, he takes her by the hand back into the sitting room and he bends her over the arm of the sofa. The sofa slowly gets moved across the room until the other side of it meets the wall, they carry on till he climaxes. She stands up and they kiss, she heads to the bathroom and he heads back into the bedroom to find some boxers just in case, he doesn't know if the kids might wake up or something after all the noise that had been made. Richard follows Nicky out to the stairs at the back of the house and she's sat there on the step, with her dressing gown wrapped around her, its cold out on the back stairs because there's no heating and its right next to the back door.

"The kids won't wake up will they? With all the...noise?" Richard asks her.

"No they are pretty heavy sleepers" she replies

"Ah right cool, I love you" he says

"I love you too "she says.

"I will give them up one day you know "she says as she sparks up a smoke.

"Give up the kids?" he asks jokingly.

"No the smokes!" she says smiling at him.

"I know you will, at your mid life crisis right?" he says.

"Yea" she laughs "are you not cold?" looking at him standing there shivering in just boxers in what must be close to freezing point. "Yea lets head back to bed and get warm" he replies. Climbing into bed he can see she has already assigned the other side of the bed to him, as in the side that's against the wall and furthest from the door. That suits him fine because he sometimes sleeps with his leg outside of the bed and if he can put it up against a wall to cool down. He puts his arms around her; she is lying with her back to his front. He kisses her on the neck and says "I love you". He starts rising to the occasion again and she can feel it.

"Yea, if you lie like this next to me I get hard straight away again" he says.

"I know, you told me before" she says.

She turns and rolls him onto his back and takes his boxers back off again. She climbs on top and kisses him. Being from Ireland he has seen some of the most beautiful scenery in the world but looking at this amazingly beautiful woman naked and on top of him with her breasts dangling in his face, all he can do is savour the moment. She gets him inside of her and he can see now that her hair is not the only wild part about her. He lets his hands wander, exploring her amazing body. He pulls her down tight against him so her ass goes in the air a bit and then he moves in and out of her real fast, she moans, she really likes that. She then takes control and rides him real hard until they both simultaneously climax. Kissing and kissing they kiss for ages. She climbs off him and rests her head on his shoulder.

"See this spot, I claim this as mine" she says.

He holds her, and soon they drift off to sleep, in each other's arms for the whole night.

In the morning they are woken up by the kids. Nicky is still quite sleepy so Richard gets up to make some coffee. He finds his way around to locate the coffee and sets up the coffee machine and switches it on. The kids walk in, looking at him.

"What you want for breakfast?" he asks them.

"Lucky charms" says Lauren.

"Hmmm ok where are they at?" Richard asks.

"I'll show you" she says. Lauren goes to the cupboard under the sink and fetches out a box of Lucky Charms and to another cupboard to get some bowls and finally spoons out of the drawer.

"Ok, I'll remember that" Richard says after taking it all in. Lauren and Gavin sit and eat their breakfast. The coffee machine is done so he makes two cups of coffee and takes one into Nicky.

"Good morning babe" Richard says, stirring Nicky as she had dropped back off to sleep.

"Thanks, you didn't have to "she says.

"I wanted to so..." he says.

"Where are the kids at?" she asks.

"Ah they are in the kitchen having their breakfast" Richard replies.

"Ok I'm getting up now" she says.

Richard returns to the kitchen, passing the kids who were on the way to the sofa and the TV. They had left a bit of a mess on the table so he starts to do the washing up and clearing the kitchen. Nicky walks past him a few minutes later, wrapped in her dressing gown and carrying her box of smokes and her cup of coffee. She gives him a weird look. Seeing him stood there at the sink was a strange thing for her. You see it was the first time she had ever seen any man stood at a sink in her whole life. Richard had spent a lot of time thinking about how he might be when he's finally here and finally around Nicky. They were people with totally differently expectations of a relationship because of the difference in culture and difference in upbringings, and even though this difference existed, it was a good thing. Let me explain. To Nicky, men are the kind that sit on the sofa, they don't help out around the house, they don't cook or clean (apart from scrubbing their own backs) and to Richard relationships to him meant something shared, yea ok men do not have a natural incline to think of all the 'cleaning things' that need to be done, however with his past relationships he had done a lot of cleaning and cooking. There was bound to be a clash here. But there was a difference in Richard too, you see in his past relationships he would do cleaning to avoid being shouted at or nagged but now he helped out because he loved Nicky.

On Monday Richard went with Nicky when she was taking Lauren to school. Her school was about a ten minute walk from the house, you have to walk up the hill which was on the street next to the house, and then down the next road, turn right and then left. The school was a big two storey white building with Canadian flags on the roof blowing in the wind. It had a play ground out the front and the grounds were surrounded by a big grey metal fence about four feet tall. A big yellow school bus came along and dropped off some children, just like you'd see happen on TV in America. Lauren was wrapped up warm in her winter coat and ran off to talk to some of her friends as soon as they got there. Nicky took Richard over and introduced him to the teacher, just so she would know who he was if he was collecting Lauren another day. From there they headed to where her dad worked. It was back past the house and then along the main road. It was a big house right on the main road; it didn't seem like a business, but as you walked inside the impression changes. It looked like a dentist's waiting room but was decorated in lots of wood so it looked old fashioned. Nicky led Richard and Gavin through to the back room. Ethan was in there with one of his employees getting some dentures ready for customers.

"Hey dad" Nicky says.

"Hey" he replies.

"Oh Rachel, this is Richard, the guy I told you about?" Introducing Ethan's employee to Richard, he nods his head in recognition and shakes her hand. She was a curly blond haired girl, 26 years old and what you would call curvy.

"Dad, can I ask a favour?"Nicky asks.

"What you mean ask a favour? Can't you see I'm working here, I can't just drop things and go just whenever you say so you know" Ethan replies, and looks at Richard and rolls his eyes. Richard smiles, sure even Richard didn't know what Nicky wanted.

"But sure dad isn't it lunch time?" knowing this would annoy him more as it was not even ten in the morning.

"No" he says

"But you don't even know what I'm asking--" Nicky says.

"Yea what is it you want this time eh, bus change? A new bed? You ain't even paid me back for the oil money yet!?" he looks at Richard again and rolls his eyes.

"No dad, I was just wondering if you'd take us up by Tim's to get some coffee..."

Ethan doesn't reply and just carries on polishing the denture that he is working on. He goes down to the basement and comes back up and attaches another tooth onto the denture. Meanwhile, Nicky just stares at him waiting for a response. After attaching the tooth, he passes it over to Rachel

"Can you finish this one off? He's coming in this afternoon for a second fitting" he says to her. Ethan then heads over to the door and picks up his jacket off the hooks.

"Come on then if we're going" Ethan says.

He drives them in his 'truck' to get coffee and gets one for himself too and for Rachel of course but he just goes to the drive through, as he wants to get back to work. Nicky and Richard headed back home with Gavin after that and relaxed at the house. Later on they collect Lauren from school and Nicky takes Richard to her Auntie Julia's house to introduce him to everyone there too. Well it got most people out of the way for 'introductions' in one day, but Richard had heard so much about everyone already, it was just putting the faces to the names now. The rest of the week flew by, Richard and Nicky didn't leave each other's sight and done everything together and they spent lots of time at night making up for a year's worth of physical distance.

Sunday morning and someone knocks at the door. Ethan walks in.

"Hey how you doing boy, you ready yet for coming out to the lake with me? ...to help get things packed for winter?" Ethan asks Richard.

"Yea just have to get dressed" Richard replies, but thinks 'this is out of the blue, and I never said that I would go anywhere with him today!'

"Ok I'll go get myself a coffee and I'll be back in about 15 and collect ya." Ethan says and disappears out the front door.

Richard walks into the bedroom and sits down next to Nicky.

"What's the story with your dad wanting me to go out to the lake with him? Should I know all about it? I'm confused" he said laughing.

"Ah he does that with any boy I'm with" Nicky says.

"Oh ok then, I best get dressed" Richard says.

Ethan is a smart guy, he likes to keep an eye on any guy that his daughter see's and maybe take advantage of their help too. Richard throws on some old clothes and gets his jacket on and he hears the horn beeping from outside so he says bye to Nicky and the kids and heads out to the 'truck'. It takes them about half hour to get out to the lake, stopping off so Richard can get some drive through coffee and a donut, which Ethan paid for, it's probably going to be his last meal, somehow he has found some axe murdering family that get people over from overseas and then kill them and bury them out by the lake house, just like in them Hollywood horrors. They call by the lake house first, Ethan shows him around. "Mr. Bell who invented the phone was a very rich man after his invention and he spent many years travelling the world before settling down and buying a place right near here because he thought it was the most beautiful place in the world" Ethan waffles off one of his little stories.

Richard thought though that given it was winter, it was pretty nice there. Ethan led him around. One goes in through the front door of the house and goes to the right there's a bedroom to your left and a bathroom to your right with a Jacuzzi bath in it, you walk out into a kitchen diner and then on a lower level the sitting room, it's all open plan and overlooking the lake. If you go back down past the bathroom and out to the other side there's another sitting room again looking onto the lake and another three bedrooms and then beyond a games room (big enough for a table tennis table) and then the back door. Beside the house then is a boat house, Ethan doesn't use this boat house for his boat though because has another one down at the land down by the lake. Anyways they get to work; Ethan lifts up a hatch on the floor by the front door which leads down to a basement crawl space. They have pieces of insulation and they cut it to size and put it around the pipes, to help prevent against freezing for the cold winter ahead. They don't chat much; they just work away and get the job done. They head off then in the 'truck' around to the lake shore which is back along the road onto the main road and then you take the next turn to the right. Ethan tells Richard all about the neighbours, who's selling who's not. Again as they pull up and get out of the truck, he shows him around the area, it's pretty steep coming down but it's a nice piece of land with trees on either side, he has a boat house and the boat is already out of the water and on the trailer, down by the lake edge is a pier and some fridges.

"David and I built that pier, sometimes you get ice bergs coming along here in winter, in fact the neighbours pier was totally destroyed by an ice berg a couple of years back" and Ethan disappears off on another set of stories. They go over to the boat after making sure the fridges were protected and they cover up the boat to protect from rain or snow. They leave when it starts to get dark and Richard gets dropped off home. Nicky must have been expecting him as dinner is nearly cooked.

"What are you cooking? It smells nice" Richard asks walking into the kitchen.

"Meatballs and spaghetti" Nicky replies.

"I've never had meatballs before" he says.

"Well you're in for a treat then cause I make the best spaghetti and meatballs" Nicky says.

Richard goes and gets changed and cleaned up and then gets called in for dinner. Sitting there at the table the four of them eat as a family. Richard nods his head with approval after the first bite.

"Can you show me how to cook this?" he asks.

"I'm not telling you my secrets to cooking!" Nicky replies.

"Ok. So when are you going to dig out the old family pictures for me to have a look at?" he says smiling. Knowing she can't refuse that one from a previous promise of doing so.

"Not tonight, maybe we could sit down tomorrow night, just the two of us, with a duvet and look through some pictures and sit and talk through things and maybe have a look at them journals too eh" Nicky says.

"Sure that sounds good to me, maybe I'll go get some beer or something and we can jus chill out and chat yea" Richard says.

"Awesome" Nicky says.

So the next day while Nicky went off to collect Lauren from school Richard went off in the direction of the alcohol shop. He had not been there yet and Nicky had only told him the general direction, but whenever he is in a new town he likes walking around because he gets to learn where things are. The biggest thing he found he needs to get used to is looking the other way when he is crossing the street, ok it seems like a small thing but he spent all his life with cars driving on the left and so looking right before crossing the road, but now he had to do the opposite. It was quite confusing so something he took his time with as he didn't want to get hit my some Canadian wondering why some silly idiot who has stepped out in front of him is looking the other way up the street. So he makes his way out away from the centre of town out towards the big shopping mall and about half way to there was an off licence as he'd call it. It was a big open plan shop and he spends a good while walking around looking at what was available. They didn't have anything he recognised from Ireland or England. He picks up some beer which Nicky had requested and he buys something called Mike's which is similar to something he used to drink back home, its vodka mixer with lemon in it. Walking back all the way to the house with two big heavy bags, Ethan passes him on the road going the opposite way and he beeps his horn. When he gets back, Nicky is already home.

"You know you could have just called for delivery" Nicky says to him as he loads the fridge.

"What you mean delivery?" he asks.

"Well it's a service, they go and collect anything you want and then deliver it to your house and you pay them, so if you want some beer and fast food, they will stop off at both for you and then deliver it to the door and they just get an extra couple of bucks to themselves" she says

'Genius' Richard thinks 'absolutely genius idea'. He pictures then that being available in Dublin where he was from, and all the tricks people would play on a service like that to get free food or beer. But in the scheme of things Canadians aren't 'chancers' like Dubliners. Nicky has some pasta cooking.

"You going to tell me your cooking secrets then?" he asks. He looks at her strangely as she throws pasta at the wall.

"No I'm not telling you the secret" she replies.

"Ok so why are you throwing pasta at the wall then?" he asks, determined to get some information on her style of cooking.

"Cause when it sticks then you know it's ready" she replies.

Hmm he thinks. It seems a bit better than his method of his taste test with a spoon which normally results in a burnt lip or finger.

"Why don't you go in and sit and watch TV while I'm cooking" she asks him as she doesn't really like spectators in her kitchen robbing her secrets. Richard goes in and sit and watches the TV, the programmes are pretty similar to what you see in Ireland, only they are released in Canada first so they get to see things in advance. He'll never be able to watch TV if he ever goes back to Ireland, because he will have seen it all already months before. So he settles on watching the 70's show, Nicky strolls in.

"Oh I love this show too" she says.

"Come lie here on sofa with me?" Richard asks her.

She lies down in front of him and he puts his arm around her waist. He could have lain there forever, but she couldn't as she was in the middle of cooking. She returns to the kitchen and before long calls him and the kids in to eat; the kids had been in their room doing their homework. After dinner, the kids get ready for bed and Nicky relaxes while Richard cleans up the dishes and the kitchen. By the time he comes in to sit down the kids are saying goodnight and heading to bed.

"So where are those photo albums then?" Richard asks.

"I'll go and try to find the photo albums and then I'll roll a joint, you go and get the duvet and some beers and some chips". Plan completed they head out to the back stairs to share the joint. Nicky didn't like to smoke in the house. Richard had never tried a joint before landing in Canada, and therefore hadn't a clue how to roll one or anything but he tried to learn her method. She would get the paper and leave it in-between cardboard in a v shape and put in some weed, and then concentrating loads. She rolls it softly between her fingers, drawing it up to her mouth she licks the edge and then twists one end to seal it, she then uses a key to push down to tighten up the contents and then breaks a bit of cardboard off her smokes packet to roll and use as a filter.

"I can smoke one without a filter, and smoke it till it's all gone" she says.

"Ya right" Richard replies. He thinks something like that must be impossible to do without burning your lip or something. Anyways they smoke the joint and go climb on the sofa, crack open a couple of beers and cuddle up under the duvet and open the photo album.

"I could only find this one; the others must be buried deep in the cupboard somewhere" Nicky says. Browsing through the pictures it was nice to see her childhood pictures; Nicky was cute even as a kid.

"Maybe one day you'll be in Ireland with me and be able to look through all my childhood pictures too" he says.

"Yea that would be awesome" Nicky says.

Photo album finished they move away from each other and sit opposite ends of the sofa, looking at each other face to face with their legs entwined under the duvet. There were some things they needed to talk about.

"Can you tell me how you can leave Ria behind, to come here to be with me?" Nicky asks.

"Well I brought my journal with me so you can read that whenever you want, it explains a lot of my thoughts about this, but basically I love Ria lots right? And I love you lots yea? I got to see Ria only 4 days and month and didn't get to see you at all, which meant for 26 days of each month I'm sat there missing the two of you, but if I am here with you then I will only miss Ria, which I would have done anyways even if I was in Ireland, I know I won't get to see her for a while, but maybe she can come over for holidays and stuff"

"Ok yea I guess I understand, you really love me don't you eh?" She asks.

"Ya of course I do, I wouldn't have come all this way if I did feel so strongly about you" he replies.

"Oh hey what happened when you left your job? You said you played some pranks? She asks.

"Oh yea, I forgot to tell you about it didn't I? Well on my last day when I got into work, I went around to all the manager's computers and on their keyboards I popped out the 'M' and 'N' keys with a screwdriver right, and then switched them. The main boss realised when he couldn't sign into his computer as N was part of his password and rang up head office IT department thinking there was some kind of computer fault but finally figured out what I had done."

"Did you get into trouble?" Nicky asks.

"No, no, he was the kind of guy who enjoys a good prank and the other managers were not there that day, so he was going to keep an eye out and have a good laugh at them too" Richard laughs.

"So is there anything you want to ask me?" Nicky asks.

Richard thinks for a few minutes, maybe he should ask about what happened in May or maybe that would not be a good idea!

"Tell me about that graveyard thing, I've always wanted to know what happened there, what that place with the cliff ..." Richard asks.

"Well me Jacob and Thomas drove out there. Thomas had been there before. We were wasted out of our faces, and so we pull up beside this big forest, and I ask which way to go and they say you got to find your own way in this life, like some spiritual bullshit. The forest can be dangerous though because there is bears strolling around. So there I am wandering through this forest, in the pitch black of night, up to knee high in mud wondering if some big bear is going to hop out and eat me. It seems liked hours but eventually I found it and met the guys there. It's an old Indian graveyard out on the edge of a cliff, and the story goes is that you stand on the edge in a certain spot and lean out and fall and a Indian spirit runs out form the forest and grabs you and pulls you back to safety. The guys lit a fire and Thomas talked me to go ahead with it, I stood right at the edge in the right spot, and closed my eyes and leaned over the edge and let go, next thing I know I was lying flat on my back on the ground looking up at the stars."

"That's mad, should I give Thomas a slap for not keeping you safe from the bears?" Richard says jokingly.

"No he told me after that he was walking nearby and was keeping an eye on me" she says.

"Ok so you never really like told me what happened between you and Jacob, I mean obviously I know about the stuff back in May and all....like how did he react when you split up with him when you got back with me?"

"You love me right? Like no matter what?" Nicky asks.

"Ya I love you no matter what" he replies but is thinking; ok what's going on, she has something to tell me that I am not going to like.

"Well it's just there are some things I have to say but it's hard for me to say it" Nicky says.

"Don't worry you can tell me anything, I love you" Richard says to reassure her even though he was starting to panic slightly.

"Ok well you know how back in July when we got back in contact and I knew it was you I wanted to be with eh?" she says.

"Ya" he replies.

"Well you know how I told you that I wouldn't see Jacob anymore? Well it's not exactly what happened, you got to understand that it's you I wanted to be with, but I guess I was just working through things. I still had something to work out of my system before I could be ready for this, to be ready to settle down with you" she says.

Richard looks away. He is unsure at how to even reply to it. His immediate reaction in his thought is that he wishes he could have known about all this before he left his daughter and travelled thousands of miles. More hurt that he was lied to than anything, as his brain starts to pull him away into thinking Nicky speaks again.

"It's you I love Richard, and I'm sorry, I wish I was stronger, and I wish you could have been here all that time".

"Can you forgive me?" she asks looking into his eyes. He

thinks for a minute, she can see the thoughts bouncing around and can almost hear his head ticking. She is expecting him to get up, get his bags and leave and maybe that is what she deserves for lying to him.

"Ok well I said I love you no matter what, I'm disappointed that you didn't finish with him when you said you did but it don't change the fact that I love you". They sit in silence for a few minutes.

"Oh hey I have something for you!" Nicky says and disappears into the bedroom and returns with a fully packed envelope and hands it to Richard.

"What's this?" he asks.

"It's the stuff I should have sent you in April, you know, the stuff you never got" she says.

Richard had always wondered what had happened to the package and opens it up, inside there's a long letter and a birthday card, as well as some pictures the kids had made for him and also a bracelet made of beads.

"They're cute" he says looking carefully at the pictures.

"What's the story with the bracelet?" he asks.

"I helped Lauren to make it for you for your birthday" Nicky says.

Richard slips it over his hand and onto his wrist.

"It's nice, thanks!" he says smiling.

"I think I'll have a read of the letter and stuff tomorrow or something, shall we head to bed babe?" he asks.

"Yea ok" she says, and they head to bed.

Good Times
Chapter 13

The next morning and Richard wakes with a distinct feeling of wishing that some of the stuff he found out the previous night had never entered his ears. In a way he felt betrayed that Nicky had carried on seeing that guy after all her promises and everything else, so he stays in the house that day, as Nicky had to go out with the kids and get a few things done. As soon as Nicky had left the house, he gets out the package that should have arrived in April and decides to have a read of the letter.

April 14th
Hey what's up? I hope that you are having a great day...I am just sitting here thinking about you...wishing so much that I could be in your arms right now...I had a dream last night...about me and you...I dreamt I was with you...It was so real and amazing...I felt so incredibly happy when I woke up this morning...I can't even put the feeling into words...but I suppose that makes no matter eh...because I know that when I come to see you...in a couple of days...(I am getting so excited)...I will feel it all over again and I won't have to find the words to tell you how I feel...I will show you and you will know...you make me feel so much...I love you...
  I really hope that you get this in time for your birthday but in case you are reading this after your birthday I hope you had an awesome birthday...I would have loved to have been able to help you celebrate...So 25 eh? It's not so bad...It's actually pretty good...I know that falling in love with you has been the best part of my 25th year... mwah infinity...Richard, I love you so much...I love everything about you...I wish you nothing but the best

for your birthday...and I hope all your birthday wishes come true...and even though I can't sing even if my life depended on it, I would sing Happy Birthday to you... make you a cake...and when the day was over i would have a little something planned...A private party just for you eh...I love you...mwah...

Well since I can't be there, I want you to know that I am thinking about you and if you close your eyes right now...think about me...can you see me? I am smiling for you...Happy Birthday Richard...I love you so much... but hey I am sure you are having a good one though... hopefully celebrating with Ria eh...you know I can't wait to meet her...and I think that me and you taking her away for a couple of days is a wonderful idea...I love you so much and I want to meet all the people in your life that you love...just as when you come to meet my family and my children...mwah...

Richard, you have my whole heart and soul...I truly know this and I do believe you are the one...the one I want to share my life with...what I feel for you is like nothing I have ever known...I can honestly say that for sure...I have never been so sure in all my life...I am smiling here...I am in awe...just wowed...amazed by you more and more every day...your amazing...I love you, I love you, I love you infinity...

It is kind of funny though when I think back to the first time we ever chatted online...even then I felt something...couldn't explain it but it made me question the possibility of what if? There was something there, there really was...I had no idea that it could develop into something this wonderful and amazing...but I can tell you this...Richard i am so thankful to have found you...I love you...I truly love you so much...I love you for you... so don't change one thing...mwah infinity...you are the most amazing man I have ever been given the chance to know...you really are...and I know this distance between us is hard at times...but not even that...not anything will ever change the way I feel about you...I will love you no matter what...I could just go on and on about how I feel for you...can't wait to be with you in a couple of days eh...weeeeeeeeeeeeeeee...I love you so much!!!

Ok so you are 25...do you feel 25? Anything yet? Ok how about now? Well I think its going to be a wonderful year for you...for us...finding you has to be the most amazing thing...Hey do you believe in wishes coming true?...Birthday wishes? I would love to see your birthday wishes come true so...I am granting you 25 birthday wishes that you may use over the next year... you can use them all at once...or space them out...but they are yours to wish...so go nuts...its all good...I love you...mwah...

Well I am going have to stop writing here...but again I hope your having a great day...and even though I can't be there for your birthday...I am there...I will be thinking about you...I love you so much...Happy Birthday...have a good one...I will talk to you soon...mwah infinity and many, many hugs and so much love
Nicky xoxoxoxox

With the letter was also a list of twenty five detailed things that Nicky loved about him. He sat there thinking about how she wrote this only days after she was raped, and weeks before she met that guy and how messed up she was at the time over everything that was going on and that it was because she needed to have someone there, someone to talk to and protect her is probably why she got with him and he cannot blame her for the fact that he could not be there! It was just something out of the control of both of them and it was all so heart breaking to the two of them of what happened, and so maybe he should just forget this guy existed and just treasure the fact that finally managed to get together and overcome all those obstacles, so that's what he decided to do.

That night and Richard and Nicky are in the bedroom lying naked on the bed. Richard has been taking his time exploring her body and had already gone down on her teasingly a few times. Richard was now laid beside her. You see, she was still shy about showing her real self in some ways, like when she hid her face under her hood of her jumper in Halifax, and Richard knew this and was trying to get through to her that she is gorgeous and amazing and that he really did love her.

"You're amazing Nicky" he says to her looking into her eyes.

"No I'm not, I'm just me" she replies.

"Yea but who you are is amazing" he says.

Nicky shakes her head, and so Richard thinks to himself for a minute, and comes up with a cunning plan. He starts kissing her, and lets his hand run down her body and he starts to play with her.

"You're amazing" he says to Nicky again and before she can reply he moves his hand just how she likes it so that she is too distracted to reply to say that she isn't this amazing person he believes her to be. He stops moving his hand.

"Well thanks, but I am just me" she finally says now that the distraction has stopped.

Richard tries again.

"You're amazing" and uses his hand again to distract her. This time he keeps going, teasing her and kissing her till she climaxes. She has forgotten to reply, success! Richard gets up and goes to the kitchen; he had been to the mall earlier in the day and bought a surprise for Nicky. It was nothing expensive and amazing; in fact it was just an ice cube tray. He knocks out the cubes into a bowl and goes back into the bedroom where she is still laid waiting for him.

"Look what I have!" smiling and showing her the contents of the bowl.

"What are you going to do with them?" she asks.

"You'll see, now you just close your eyes" he says.

She closed her eyes. He puts an ice cube in his mouth. He starts to kiss her neck and then works his way down her body slowly, letting the ice cube in his mouth slowly cool down his mouth, tongue and lips. Richard loves to tease, but he had never tried this one before. After teasing her for a while, he goes ahead and starts using his tongue between her legs; she jumps a little.

"Oh my god, wow, that feels nice" she says to him.

"Yea can you feel my cold tongue and all?" he asks as he lifts his head momentarily to get a new ice cube. He carries on pleasuring her until she climaxes. After he lies on the bed beside her again and she climbs on top of him, she pulls him up so he is sitting too, and they start to make love, lots of kissing, and she gets noisy, as was normal for them. They hear a loud bang on the ceiling coming from above.

"It must be Emma banging on her floor" Nicky says.

You know how sometimes having sex in a public place can be quite exciting, but it's something different when its family that can hear you. So they try to keep it quiet but Nicky loses her cool because she can't be herself. Emma is actually a bit jealous of what the two of them have, her boyfriend is never around much and she's just sat up there by herself doing nothing most of the time. Anyways they get up off the bed and throw on a few bits of clothing and go out to the back staircase. Nicky lights up a smoke.

"Who does she think she is eh" she says loudly, loud enough for Emma to hear it echo up the stairs.

"Don't worry about it, just ignore her ok?" he says to her to try and calm the situation down a bit.

"But like I can't, I want to be me and yea I am noisy but it's who I am and I don't want to be worrying about being too loud or any----"

He kisses her. He runs his hand between her legs, next thing they know they are having sex there and then on the bottom of the stairs.

"Keep it in the fucking bedroom" they hear Emma shout, followed by some loud banging coming from the room at the top of the stairs. So that's exactly what they did, they headed back to the bedroom and made as much noise as they could. It wasn't long before Emma started kicking the floor from above again. Nicky had enough. She threw on some clothes and stormed off out the front of the house. Richard was left lying there thinking that this is going to get ugly. He hears mumblings then banging and shouting. Nicky comes in not long after.

"I broke her door" she says laughing.

"Well Emma's boyfriend John broke it already and she tried to fix it with some tape, and well I kind of put my foot through it now" she says.

Richard laughs; he thinks it's pretty funny.

"I need a smoke" she says.

Funny that isn't it, how when something stressful happens a smoke solves everything. Well it didn't quite solve this. About twenty minutes later Ethan comes by the house.

"What's this about you breaking Emma's door Nicola?" Ethan asks.

"I didn't break it, her fella did" Nicky replies.

"Well did you go up there kicking at it and shouting?" Ethan asks.

For a moment they stop talking and stare at each other.

"I can't handle this I'm going for a smoke" and Nicky walks off from Ethan to the back door.

Ethan looks at Richard, looking to aim his anger somewhere, 'Oh shit oh shit I'm in trouble here' Richard thinks to himself.

"Look" Ethan says

"I don't care if you two fuck like rabbits but can you two keep the noise down in the bedroom please?" Ethan says with an angry face.

"Yea sure" Richard replies, sure what else could he say, it was just to keep Ethan happy, He leaves, slamming the door behind him. Richard goes out to the back stairs where Nicky is puffing away on a cigarette.

"He's after asking me to keep the sex quieter!" he says to Nicky.

"What? That's insane; I'm going to kill Emma" she says.

"Ah leave it for tonight, maybe we should just head off to bed yea, it's after two now anyways" he says to calm her down.

She stares at the floor for a minute and finishes her smoke. "Yea ok" she says. They go back to bed and try to get some sleep. Richard, lying there is thinking about that phone call Ethan must have received from Emma. "Dad can you come down here and tell them two to stop having such loud sex, and while you're at it, ask her why she kicked my door down". It's so different to the family he had grown up with that's for sure!

On Sunday Ethan calls by again. It seems that the other night never happened although no words are exchanged between Nicky and her dad. Richard knew the score by this time so he grabs his jacket and goes with Ethan. They make few stops on the way out to the lake; they pick up Thomas on the way and also scaffolding to get onto the roof. That was the plan for the day, Ethan's carpenter friend, who was one of the lake neighbours was meeting them there too to help fix up the roof.

"So why are we fixing the roof, is it leaking?" Richard asks Ethan.

"No, it's not leaking but it needs doing cause I want to sell the house and you can see it needs doing from the outside, I just hope the shingle that we replace looks the same as the rest of the roof, as I don't want to do the whole roof" he says.

Richard nods his head along with Ethan wanting to keep to conversation away from the topic of the other night.

"So what did you do last night" Richard asks, as the shingle conversation was dying off.

"I was on a date last night" Ethan says.

"Yea? How did that go?" Richard asks.

"Well we went for a meal and then went back to mine. She was good looking, had nice big tits. She had long hair though, and this morning there was like long black hairs all over the house, maybe I shouldn't see girls with long hair" Ethan says.

Richard already regretting asking the first question as that was way too much information decides to move away from the sex side of things.

"So you going to see her again?" he asks

"Ah I'm not sure, she's got kids and, well I've done the whole raising kid's thing now twice and I don't really want to go through all that again." Ethan replies.

"So you don't believe in soul mates and stuff?" Richards asks.

"No no, there's no such thing as love, there's only companion-ship" Ethan replies.

Richard drifts off into his thoughts and thinks that it's easy for Ethan to say that as he's been through two family set ups and has achieved any fulfilments within those times so now he doesn't have to worry about love and children, but it's unfair for Ethan to say that to him knowing that he has travelled half way across the world to be with Nicky in the belief of one thing, love, so how can love not exist? How can there only be companionship?

When they arrive at the lake, they unpack the scaffolding around to the front end of the house and Richard and Thomas start setting it all up ready for the job ahead. It was cold that day, it had previously been snowing so the ground had a couple of inches of snow on it and it was about minus 6 degrees Celsius. Ethan's neighbour John arrives, he is an old guy, must be retired with that amount of grey hair but he does have a full head of hair and is well built but a bit chubby.

They all climb up on the roof with a hammer each, they start by pulling off some of the damaged section of the roof and John then replaces any damaged joist before moving onto the next section, and then Richard and Thomas hammer in the new shingles. It's very different roofing to Ireland, they use slates there. Anyways they crack on with the job on top of this roof in one of the most gorgeous places in the world looking out onto the lake, Richard didn't care that it was cold, it was beautiful there. He'd buy the house if he had the money to do so! With the work they were doing they could only really wear the one glove though but Richard's hands don't get cold, his ears get cold quite quickly and he hates when his ears are cold. They finish after a couple hours of hard labour and Ethan steps back from the house to have a good look, the colour of the replacement shingles they put up didn't look so different to what was there already so it was a good job done. They go for lunch in a local sea food restaurant and then they go over to John's house which is just down the road from Ethan's lake house. Ethan and John go into the house, probably sorting out a bit of business between them or something. Thomas spots a deer down below by the lakeside.

"Quick go in and tell them there's a deer" Thomas says to Richard.

So Richard goes inside and gives the guys a shout.

"You saw deer?" John asks Thomas as he comes outside.

"Yea they went off that way, at least three of them" said Thomas pointing to the forest area to the left of the lakeshore. Ethan and John fetch their rifles out from under their seats in their 'trucks' and head off down to chase the deer to try and shoot one. Thomas takes a few sneak looks to make sure they are gone and he rolls a quick joint and shares it with Richard. They hear a couple of loud bangs, and decide to go down to see what's going on. They run down the hill towards the forest area. Ethan calls them over, he's about 100 yards into the forest, and so they scramble through the heavy forest and find him standing over a body of a deer.

"You see the bullet hole there, and there's the other one" Ethan says as he lifts up the leg.

"I injured it in the leg first then I got a good shot at it, I had thought it had got away but then there it was standing looking at me" he says and you can almost see the adrenalin running through his veins.

"If you drag it back to the boat house, there might even be a steak in it for you" he adds.

Grabbing a horn each Richard and Thomas drag the heavy carcass back through the forest, stopping now and then to free the legs as they get caught up in the branches and roots. The blood was dripping everywhere too and Richard was trying not to get that all over him. After they get it out in the open John and Ethan help they carry it up the hill into the boathouse. John ties its rear feet to a strong rope and the four of them to heave it up into the air, and John ties the rope off.

"You got a knife?" John asks Ethan but he shakes his head.

"Ok I'll run up to the house" and he returns with what one would call a pen knife, you know the ones with red handles and multiple tools on them.

"What are you going to do with that?" Richards asks as he has never seen a dead deer before and was quite shocked that John hadn't brought back a big knife.

"Well we have to gut it now and then leave it hanging for a couple of days" Ethan informs him as John proceeds to cut open the belly of the deer,

"The trick is, to get the bladder out without bursting it, because if that burst then it will spoil the meat" John says as he cuts away at the deer. There's no way that you can describe the smell of a deer's guts. It really is a disgusting smell and the sight wasn't much better. It stank. Richard was glad when he was asked to go fetch a bucket to put the guts into. He brought the bucket back and left them to it, the smell was too much for him, and well the whole experience had really left him in shock, probably didn't help with the fact he was stoned, and sure Thomas was stoned too, so they would share the odd glance off into space. With the deer all gutted and Ethan happy they head back to Sydney as it was getting dark. Richard sits there in the truck listening to their hunting stories, Thomas likes to go up in a tree and wait on a perch for a deer to come walking by, and Ethan once seen one on the road and he pulled in, shot it, and threw it in the back of the truck. Richard's stoned thoughts started thinking about how Ethan has a gun and what would he do if he ever became unhappy with him, Canada is such a vast space, a buried body would never be found, and sure Nicky would think he just went home to Ireland, And everyone in Ireland would think he has moved on and can't be bothered with anyone back there, and that would be the end of him. Paranoia I know, kids stay off them drugs.

When Richard got back to the house, he was feeling in the mood for a bit of fun with Nicky though the kids were still up. He goes into the kitchen and sees Nicky standing at the kitchen sink, he stands behind her and start kissing her neck and slips his hand down the front of her jeans and starts to tease her. She starts biting her lip as she knows she can't make a noise because the kids are in the next room. She takes him by the hand and leads him to the bathroom and shuts the door, locking it so the kids can't come in. Nicky proceeds to unzip her jeans and take them off, as Richard does with his. He then lifts her up onto him with her ass half resting on the radiator and they start having wild sex, they just can't wait till later. Nicky gives up biting her lip and so they both start getting carried away with things. Lauren starts knocking at the door saying "mammy", Nicky refuses to let Richard stop and they carry on for a few minutes till they both climax. They walk out of the bathroom, as if nothing has happened. Lauren frowns at them. Too young to understand what they were up to.

Later that Night they are cuddled up to each other in their bed.

"Tell me a story, it will help me sleep" she says to him. Richard thinks for a few minutes to think of something to start a story about.

"Once upon a time there was a Tomato. He lived in the fridge with all the other tomatoes. But he even though it was quite nice there, he noticed every now and again one of his friends or family would go missing and he'd never see them again. So he always wondered what was up with this world and he had a very strong intention to find out somehow. But he looked around and is surrounded by a fully enclosed box and knew to himself he would never get an opportunity. One night however he was woken from his sleep, opening his little red eyes, he seen the box was open, someone must have left it open. He rolls himself forward and out of the fridge, as quietly as possible so as not to wake up any of the other Tomatoes. He spends a while rolling around the floor, its cold and dark out here, after a while he gets tired and takes a nap. The house owner wakes up the morning and closes the fridge realising that he had left it open after his late night snack. This was his cleaning day and he starts sweeping up the kitchen only to discover a Tomato lying there on the fridge floor. O he thought to himself, I must have knocked it out of the fridge last night when I was half asleep. He sweeps it up with the rest of the floor dust and drops it in the kitchen. As the Tomato falls and hits the rubbish inside it has woke him up from his sleep, unaware of the danger that he was in. He looks around; he's surrounded by foul smelling trash. Next thing he knows the light goes out and he can feel that he is moving and then comes to a sudden stop. He lies there in shock for a while thinking how do I get out of this mess, all I wanted to do is see beyond the box I have been in for so long."

Richard looks at Nicky thinking she is asleep by now, she opens her eyes and looks at him "what happens next?" she asks.

"Well the Tomato realises then that there is a rip in the big and he rolls himself across and out of the rubbish bag to find him at the bottom of the garden. It's sunny out and he is really far away from the house and he can't really go strolling around out in the open, someone might see him. He waits for it to get dark and then he rolls out across the finely cut grass towards the house, once he reaches the door he realises he can't get in, and so lying there tired after his trip across the garden he drops off to sleep. In the morning he wakes just in time to dodge out of the way as the door opens, looking up and realising he hasn't been seen he rolls back inside the kitchen just before the door closes behind him. Glad to be nearly home to his friends he finds a quiet spot to hide and to think at how to get back in the box." He looks at Nicky again, she's fast asleep. Lying there with her head on his shoulders, he thinks back to that moment back in May when she broke his heart and how he'd believe that this moment would never happen, and here he was. The light of the moon is shinning in the window so he lay there for a while looking at her until he too drifts off into his dreams.

Things Get a Little
Chapter14

The weekend was coming around; it was Richard's third weekend in Canada. The last couple weekends David hadn't turned up to take the kids for the weekend. The weekends were David's scheduled time to have the kids each week and so Richard and Nicky hadn't had the chance to go out together on the town. So they had a plan to go out on Friday, as long as David turns up this time. David showed up and was only a half hour late but at least he collected the kids this time. Nicky stuck on some tunes to listen to while they got ready to go out. Richard was ready well before she was, as you'd expect so he sat on the sofa chilling out. When Nicky was all done and ready to go, she came out of the bedroom, ok its always Richard's belief that she looked beautiful without any make up but now she was all done up and she was looking really hot. Nicky checks she has her ID with her, even though she knew some of the people working at the bars, they would always ID her, and Richard brought his too. It saves coming back to the house for it later! They walk around to her Auntie Julia's house first and they sit there in the kitchen. Thomas is there and they open up some beers that they brought with them from the fridge and enjoy a joint with Thomas. It was weird for Richard to see people smoking weed around their parents, it must be a Canadian thing, not that I am saying all Canadians are this way at all. Anyways they get on our way to being drunk and stoned and then head off down to the pool hall which is half way between Nicky's house and town centre. For a long time Nicky had told Richard how good she is at playing pool and can do all the tricks and all. The pool hall is down in the basement and has about six tables and a small bar. Richard orders in some beers while Nicky lines up the balls on the table. He lets her break and then it's his shot. He is not that great at pool and holds the cue totally the wrong way but he does get the odd Lucky shot like getting in two balls in one go. They play a few games and he wins two out of three, so much for Nicky's skill, or maybe it was the Irish luck that won it. At this point they are at the merry stage of getting drunk, they leave the pool hall and stand at edge of the main road trying to flag down a taxi into town, even though its only a ten minute walk away, it's only ten minutes when you're sober and walking. Richard had been practicing taking the Mick out of Canadian accents by copying some Canadian TV stars so he stands there making impressions and making Nicky laugh. A taxi pulls up and Nicky tells him where to drop them off in town. It was still early in the night, it was only around ten.

Walking into the first club there's no queue, probably because it's still so early in the night. They walk up stairs, which are broken in the middle by a landing on the way up.

"Hi" Nicky says to a woman that passes them on the stairs, the woman doesn't reply and just walks by. The woman is short and blonde and slightly chubby and in her forties. Nicky links arms with Richard and pulls him over and puts her lips to his ear.

"That's the woman who runs this place, she doesn't really like me much" she whispers to him

"How come?" he asks Nicky.

"She a friend of David's family" she replies.

They go in and order a drink at the bar and then find a seat. The place is pretty empty, only about another ten people in there and the bar staff is still setting up for the night ahead. They have some general music playing; the DJ is not on yet or anything. Nicky can't wait to dance so she drags Richard up onto the dance floor and they are the only two up on the dance floor. They dance to some R&B songs and love it; Richard is not a great dancer so always enjoys dancing more when someone is dancing with him. Their dancing to anyone looking would have looked a lot like two people making love on the dance floor, as it was quite sexual you could say. Richard noticed that woman who Nicky said hello to, is now behind the bar and was giving them some very bad looks across the bar. Richard seen her talking to the people on the bar then but he didn't care what about until he went to order another round of drinks.

"I'm sorry we can't serve you anymore" the barman said.

Richard looks around and there's no sight of the blond woman anymore. Nicky is unaware of the situation and is sat back at the seats they had picked out, recovering from their dancing session.

"Why can't you serve us anymore?" Richard asks.

"Cause you've had enough" he says but his eyes drift over looking at Nicky, pointing out that he 'thought' that Nicky had enough and not him.

"That's a load of crap" he says to the barman and walks off.

Richard walks back over to Nicky who is sat there looking at him and wondering why he doesn't have drinks in his hand.

"Come on, we better go, they won't let me order anymore drinks!" Richard says to her.

She frowns at him.

"Well they think we have had enough, the only thing I have

had enough of is the dirty looks from that blond woman" he says in his usual cheekiness.

Nicky puts her jacket back on and they make their way to the door, escorted out by the eyes of the barman and the blond who had mysteriously re-appeared. They walk out across the car park which is directly facing the other bar they are heading to next. Nicky falls over on the ground and Richard scrambles to help her up and sit her down on the edge of the wall.

"Are you ok?" he asks her

"Yea, just give me a minute" she says, as she comes to terms with how much alcohol she has actually drank, and looks at Richard who still seems pretty sober to be fair and wondering if he has secretly been drinking water instead. When she has had a few minutes they join the queue to get into the club but when they get to the bouncers, they refuse to let them in. 'Damn it they must have seen Nicky fall over' Richard thinks to himself.

"What you want to do now? You wanna head home?" Richard asks her, knowing she is already quite drunk.

"No I want to go on to Herman's bar, it's the best one anyways, save the best for last eh" Nicky says.

"Ok... which way is it from here?" He asks.

Nicky holds his hand and leads him around the back of the bar they had just tried to get into and down a little grassy area; she loses her footing and falls down dragging him with her. The two of them lie there on the ground laughing their heads off. Richard gets up and helps her to her feet. She's grabs his arm tight now as they walk so that she doesn't fall over again. They get across the grass bit and then walk up the street to the bar. Immediately as they go in he likes the place, it's got a nice big bar and then a big dance floor and a big stage for bands to play and a balcony over the far side for the smokers.

"I can see why this is the best place in town" he says.

"Yea well you've been everywhere now boy" she says.

They go to the bar and after several requests Richard finds a drink that they have that he recognises. They down a few drinks and shots at the bar. This place is much busier than the other places. One of the local bands is playing that night; a lot of people are there just to see them play. They get out on the dance floor and start dancing away, same as they had in the first place, except by this time they were more drunk and definitely crazier on the dance floor. Nicky falls down flat on her back on the floor, but just carries on dancing there on the ground where she fell.

"Why don't you go get a room" they hear some other random person dancing say to them. So they head off to the bar again, Nicky trips up the stairs. They get more drinks and they're really enjoying the band playing and the night, so they get back out onto the dance floor. It's not long before Richard feels someone grab his arm, it's a bouncer.

"I think you two have had enough and I think you should leave" he says. Another bouncer joins him and they get removed from the bar and escorted out the front door. Standing outside, Nicky's dying for a smoke but hasn't got any left. Richard flags down a taxi. Nicky clambers into the back and Richard follows, she sits and stares out the window for a minute while Richard gives the driver the address for home. She remembers suddenly how much she wants a smoke.

"Hey can we stop at the garage eh? She asks the driver. The driver nods his head.

The taxi pulls up in the yard of the petrol station, the meter is still running and the driver is not very happy to have been asked to stop. This was his busiest night and he was eager to get back into town as soon as he could.

"What you want?" Richard asks.

"Erm, well get me a pack of smokes, and..... yea also get me some Doritos, you know, the cool ones"

Noticing Richards frown she informs him "they're the ones in the blue packet eh" and smiles.

Richard gets out and spends some time walking around before finding everything, although it was a small list, he wasn't the best at finding things easily with or without alcohol. Richard passes the stuff to Nicky when he returns to the taxi, and she immediately pulls out a smoke and proceeds to open the window and light it up.

"Hey you don't mind do you..." she asks looking to the driver and he shakes his head in annoyance. He must be one of those drivers that stays quiet but curses you when you leave. When the taxi gets to the house, Richard gets out followed by Nicky and she scrambles up the porch steps while he settles the bill with the driver. She slips and nearly falls but recovers and laughs to herself, reaching the top she stops and waits for Richard to follow her and open the door. As soon as she walks into the sitting room she collapses on the floor.

"Damn it Nicky I can't leave you there, come on, come get into bed" he says.

"No I don't want to, I'm good here" she says.

"Don't' be stupid, you can't sleep there" he says with a little laugh looking at her on the cold wood floor.

He helps her into the bedroom, half carrying her and half dragging her and lifts her onto the bed. As he leans over her she opens her eyes again momentarily and kisses him.

"Make love to me" she says.

"No, you sleep it off" he says but she has already gone asleep again so he climbs over her onto the other side of the bed and falls asleep too.

This was an important week ahead as it was going to be Nicky's birthday on Wednesday. Nicky was still going to school but she was struggling more and more to get out of the bed in the mornings. Richard was first awake on Monday.

"You want me to take Lauren to school?"

"And then you can stay in bed a little longer?" he asked Nicky.

"Yea ok" she replied.

"Lauren "Nicky shouted

Lauren comes in and stands to attention beside the bed.

"Your clothes are in your bedroom all ready for school; Rich's going to take you this morning" Nicky says to her.

Richard goes out to the kitchen and help the kids get their breakfast. He takes a coffee into Nicky and leaves it beside the bed; it looks like she's gone back to sleep. He already knew the 'bring Lauren to school routine' as he had been plenty of times with Nicky to drop Lauren off or collect her and the teachers knew his face by now. This was the first time he had taken Lauren by himself though. He looked out the window; it must have snowed last night.

"Lauren you'll need your snow boots on today and your coat and hat and scarf and gloves" he says to her.

The snow plough had been along at some part of the night as the snow was all heaped up against the house. That's a great idea to clear the road, but it doesn't help with being able to get out of your house if there is six foot of snow piled up. The path had frozen over and was really slippery too. "Come on Lauren, we need to go now or you'll be late" he says to hurry her along.

He helps her on with her jacket and they walk off up the road. He didn't have very good foot wear and was sliding all over the place. He'd step forward and slide back as they walked up the hill. It wasn't too bad after the hill and they got there in one piece.

"Ok Lauren, I'll see you later, have a good day at school" he said to her as she ran off to get a few minutes of play time with her friends in the snow before going into class. Richard waited until the teachers brought the kids inside and then he walked off down towards the mall. He wanted to have a look around at what he might be able to get Nicky for her birthday. He has a quick walk through to see what's on offer. He sees a big make up thing that folds out. 'Nicky will love that' he thought to himself. It was 50 dollars, he bought it there and then and headed back to the house, he didn't want to be too long as he wanted her birthday things to be a surprise. When he got home he hides the make-up set, knowing he can wrap it when Nicky is at college tomorrow.

"Hi Gavin, is your mum up yet?" Richard asks.

"No she's still in bed" Gavin replies.

He goes in to check on her and she's lying awake in bed. She never drank the coffee; she had not woken up before it had got cold. Richard sits on the bed beside her.

"Laurens at school ok, you should see the roads outside, super slippy" he says laughing.

"Thanks for taking her, I really didn't feel like I could get up this morning" she says.

"That's ok babe" He replies.

"I love you Rich" she says smiling at him.

"I love you too" he says.

"Gavin" Nicky shouted.

"Come up here" she says to him when he comes in and he climbs on the bed. She grabs him and tickles him and starts playing and joking with him.

"Ok I'm going to go make some fresh coffee ok?" Richard says to her and goes to the kitchen. It was a slow day and after making coffee he grabs Nicky's laptop which was free and logged on to check his emails, there was one there from his mum asking how things were going. He replied telling her a few things like the lake and things and asked her to send some custard, as they don't have custard here in Canada and you know how when you know you can't have something, how much more you want it. He downloads some games then to the laptop and then Gavin seen them and wanted a turn. It was soon time to go collect Lauren so he went by himself to go collect her. The paths were still as slippery as ever but he got there and back without falling over.

The next day he does the school trip again except he brought Gavin along with him, Nicky had gone off to school. When he gets back to the house he takes advantage of the quiet house to get everything ready for Nicky's birthday tomorrow. He had arranged for Thomas to get some weed too for her for her birthday so they could have a joint. Anyways leaving Gavin playing away on the games on the laptop, he writes out a card and wraps Nicky's present and then hid it somewhere where she wouldn't go looking, which was in his green bag which was still sat on the bedroom floor. He done a quick clean up around the house and cleaned up the dishes from breakfast and made the bed. After that he sat down with Gavin and they took turns on the games.

"Hey what you think about when we go and collect Lauren that we make some birthday cards for your mum for Tomorrow" Richard says to Gavin.

"Aw can we not make them now?" Gavin asks.

"No, no we are going to get Lauren in ten minutes so we could all just do them together when she is here too" Richard replies. He let him have the last go on the game and then they collect Lauren from school and they explain the plan to her on the way back.

"Right ok, where do you keep paper?" Richard asks Gavin and Lauren.

"Oh over here" Lauren goes over to this hexagon shaped table and opens up a little door that's on the front of it, Richard hadn't realised it even had a door! Ok so he gives them a few ideas, and they go for having something pop up inside the card when it opens and he shows them how to make it.

"Ok so are you going to give these to your mum in the morning?" he asks them.

"Yea we'll go in and wake her up and then give her the card" Lauren says.

"Ok then, well you best go and hide them in your bedrooms somewhere" he tells them so Nicky won't find them.

"Lauren have you got any homework to do?" Richard asks her.

"No not today" she says.

"Well then do you guys want to play on the computer?" he asks but it's a silly question, the real question was how long would it go before they would be arguing over whose go it is on the games he had downloaded. Richard starts tidying up after the craft time. There are lots of bits of paper and crayons and markers which he starts throwing back into the hexagon table. On one of the pieces of paper he notices something. There's writing on it and it looks like Nicky's, checking to see if the kids have seen him find it, they haven't. He takes it quietly and goes into the bedroom and reads it. He feels bad reading it, as if it wasn't meant for his eyes. He realises straight away its some sort of love letter or diary note that Nicky had written in reference to Jacob and how she felt about him. It confused him, he didn't realise that she had loved him, and thought that their relationship had just been like a summer fling kind of thing, a bit of fun to pass time. Now he knew different. He thinks about asking Nicky about it, but doesn't want to be accused of snooping, then thinks about putting it back, but he didn't want the kids to find it, and in the end he puts it with his personal stuff on his shelf area in the wardrobe, well hidden, and has no intention to mention it for now. He opens up his guitar case, and start strumming away and then singing, just some of his own tunes that he had written before, in order to try and chill out after his discovery. Lauren walks in. "Is that your own song?" she asks.

"Yea it is" he answers and stops playing.

"I wish I could make up songs" she says.

"Ah it's actually quite easy, here I'll show you" he says and invites her to sit down.

"Ok so what do you want to have the song about?" he asks her.

"Errrm, what about the cat?" Lauren replies.

"Yea ok sure, ok so first you need a tune and then you just make it up as you go along" he says.

Strumming a few chords he makes a song "the crazy cat, its sits by the window all day, it's never been outside and it thinks that the windows a TV" Lauren laughs.

"You see it's not so hard is it" Richard says to her. Gavin joins them.

"Can I have a go?" Lauren asks. He passes the guitar across to her and shows her how to hold the guitar and she has a go at strumming the strings so he shows her the easiest chord which is E-minor. He has given people lessons in the past, he's not qualified as you would say but experienced enough to guide people would be a more accurate way to explain it. As with any musical instrument, the main thing is practice. The kids run off again to their computer and he puts the guitar away.

Wednesday arrives but more importantly its Nicky's birthday. Richard and Nicky wake up pretty early and knowing that the kids would be up soon they get a sneaky bit of fun in, well it is her birthday and that's the best way to start it off. The kids come in soon after, and Nicky loves the home made cards that the kids made for her. Richard climbs up out of the bed and goes to the bathroom. Nicky gets up and makes the kids some breakfast and sticks on the coffee maker which is priority in the morning. Richard gets her present from its hiding spot and brings it into Nicky in the kitchen. Un-wrapping it like a 5 year old on Christmas morning, she looks confused and then realises what it is.

"Aww I've always wanted one of these" she says. She had told him before she had wanted one but that was ages ago and she hadn't expected him to get it for her for her birthday.

Once some coffee has been drunk they all take Lauren to school together.

"There's a party on this Saturday at Julia's, well my cousin Luke is coming back from out west for a while and it's his 18th birthday so I was thinking we could go to that? It'll be like a combined party for me and him" Nicky says to Richard.

"Sounds good to me" he says as he is never one to miss a good party. Partly Nicky just wanted to go so she could show off her new makeup. The party was at Julia's and when they arrived they joined everyone down in the basement. There was a nice big room down there and a toilet and a make shift bar, but it was a 'bring your own beer' kind of party. Some other guys arrive and they are passing around the joints like you wouldn't believe, one guy rolls a cigar which was just solid weed with some of that black resin stuff broken into it too. That was then passed around the room and in-between there was smaller joints going round too. The whole room was just like a big cloud of smoke. Richard had drank lots too and dosed off for a nap, but it must have been a power nap because he woke up with loads more energy and kept on partying then. It was a good night, they had fun.

That Sunday afternoon though they were struggling to get out of bed.

"There's something we need to talk about" Nicky says.

"Ok babe, what's up?" he asks.

"I think I'm pregnant" she says. Richard stares off into space for a minute just letting it soak in. "Well hey that's ok Nicola, I love you and no matter what we can do this right" he says.

Nicky looks down, and says "I don't think I want the baby"

Richard doesn't know what to think, it's not the reaction he expected and something that went against his beliefs.

"Well we got some time to think about don't we?" he says.

"Yea I guess, and I don't even know for sure yet, I need to do a test, can you go buy one?" She asks him.

"Yea ok" he says. He throws on some clothes and heads off down to the nearest shop. His thoughts were racing with the news 'I love Nicola and I support her no matter what' he starts thinking 'but why doesn't she want it?' and he carries on thinking. Nicola's thoughts were somewhat different though, she was sat at the house thinking too. Unknown to Richard, the night out where she had got wasted and fell all over the place, well you see, she had woke up the next day and not really remembered the night before, she had marks on her body from falling and she only had her underwear on (she had taken off the rest of her clothes in the night) but it had brought back memories of when she had been raped and, she thought something had happened that night too, and her trust in Richard was slowly disappearing and now, if she is pregnant, well she is already freaking out to say the least. Richard arrives back with the test and she takes it and goes into the bathroom. Richard sits on the sofa and watches the clock hands slowly move, and it seems like forever but Nicky returns to confirm that she is indeed pregnant.

"Look Nicola, I love you with all my heart and I would have this baby with you and support you and whatever you need" he says to her.

"But I'm not sure I want it Richard" she says as if his words had bounced back off the wall she was building around herself. David drops the kids back, worst timing ever when they are in such a deep conversation.

"I think I am going to go for a walk" Richard says and he heads off down to the boardwalk in town which is really quite nice in the evening or night time. He starts to think, starts to analyse, why doesn't Nicky want their baby. Maybe it's because David her ex had treated her so bad and maybe she feels like he might turn out to be the same, or maybe because it's because it will mess up her education. She plans to do her last year in college next year and that will mess it all up for her. Maybe it's a mix of those two reasons. Richard continued to think on and decided that that must be why and therefore if he can somehow reassure her that he can be there for her and that he's different to David and that he will support her so she wouldn't have to give up school well than maybe she might be ok about this. Nicky however sat at the house, wondering what Richard is out and thinking about, starts to think do I really want a kid with this guy, look what happened when we went out, and well he's only been here a month and how well do I really know the guy.

Broken Hope
Chapter15

    Richard had become friends with one of Nicky's friends Rachel which was the girl who worked for Nicky's dad. She had same name as his best friend Rachel in England, the funny thing was that this Rachel in Canada, well her best friend was called Richard too. Anyways Rachel played gigs with her band in the pubs and clubs around the area, and she knew that Richard was a bit of a singer song writer. She invited him to a singer song writer night in a local pub; the fee taken at the door gets split between the artists there so you can get between 5 dollars and seventy dollars, depending on how busy it is there of course. Richard wanted Nicky to come along, you know for the support and for good memories and all that. He asked Nicky, you know have a few drinks and a laugh but she didn't want to come, maybe she just wanted some time to herself to think about things, besides there was no child minder to look after the kids anyways. So Richard heads off down there going by the direction he had been given and he found it eventually. It wasn't too far from the tar pit. Ok the tar pit for those who don't know the story of this little town, well many years ago there used to be a steel plant and they polluted the local river and lake so much it turned into a solid mass of chemical waste, and there has been malformed births and everything from the pollution, it's all boarded off but they say if you throw a rock in it, it will just sit on the top, even though you can't get to see it, if the wind blows a certain way you can definitely smell it. The pub was smaller than what Richard had expected it to be. All the musicians got the chance for a quick sound check, Richard's guitar wasn't coming through very well so it had to be turned up to the max, After panicking for a few minutes he got it to a point where he could use it, but it didn't sound great. There was four of them playing that night and he was up third, he played a set of 5 songs, one of which he had only just written the week before. It went pretty well and he got twenty dollars for playing which covered the beers he had drank, well hey a free night out that's a good thing!? Ok it would be great if he could find a normal job and earn some money, He had not been able to find anything yet and well the money he has brought with him will not last forever.

Richard went for a walk the next day; he needed to think about things and walking helps him think. He was still panicking a bit about the whole situation as things at the house are gradually getting worse; Nicky seems more and more agitated with him. He stops off in the music shop and play the guitars they have there for a while, playing the guitar always calms him. On the way back he stops at a local jewellery shop, it had been in his mind that he would like to ask Nicky to marry him, and even though they had talked about that kind of stuff before he came over, he had a sudden thought that maybe he should ask her on Christmas day. It might help settle things down and show her that he is there to support her and that he really does love her. When Richard gets home there's a package waiting for him, it's the custard he had asked his mum to send him, and a little letter from her too and also some Christmas presents for him and for Nicky and for the kids too which was a nice surprise, and Nicky was surprised too. Nicky loves all things Christmassy. In the letter his mum wrote about Ria. His mum and Dad had arranged to see Ria for the day and travelled up to collect her and brought her to their house for the day. Ria had rushed around when she got to the house. Ria was looking for her dad. Richard's mum said to her "your daddy has gone on the airplane and pointed out the window towards the sky, but Ria didn't understand and said "no daddy in nana's home". His mum goes on to tell him how Ria is missing him and how she is now getting potty trained and she came along with her potty. She's growing up so fast. It made him sad thinking about Ria there without him and he did miss her a lot, but there's not much he can do about that right now. He decided to give the custard a try as Nicky and kids had never had it before. He cooked some bread and butter pudding to go with it. Now this is one of his favourite desserts and the kids liked it but Nicky didn't like it so much, she couldn't taste it from all the years of her smoking eroding her taste buds. She was surprised that he was even able to cook such a thing.

12th of December is the magical date where people put their Christmas decorations up. Richard was given instructions to go with Ethan down to pick out a tree. When they got there, well Richard was nervous at which one to get, Christmas is such a big thing for Nicky and the last thing he wanted to do was to bring back a tree that was no good. After having a good browse around he asks Ethan which one he should go for, Ethan was quite reluctant to help him pick one, probably for the same reasons that Richard was struggling to pick one. In the end he just went with the one that looked the best to him, considering it was really dark out (the tree sellers probably don't have lights on purpose!). He gives the guy the twenty bucks and Ethan gives him a hand to throw it in the back of the truck. On the way back to the house Richard decides to talk to Ethan about Nicky.

"I hope Nicky likes the tree!?" Richard says.

"She should, it's a good one eh" Ethan says.

"Erm...you know I love Nicky a lot, like to move over here and all to be with her" Richard says.

"Well yea, but there's only really companionship you know?"

Ethan says.

"I know that's what you believe but I believe in love and well...well I would like to ask Nicky to marry me" Richard says and turns to look at Ethan.

"Well... That's all well and good, but you should consider just companionship" Ethan says laughing. Richard says no more, as Ethan wasn't taking him seriously.

When Richard got back to the house it was all out of his hands, Nicky would not let anyone do any Christmas decorations, and she let the kids help of course. It was like a whirlwind watching her run around decorating the whole house, the only job Richard got was to help untangle the Christmas lights. The tree looked awesome sitting in the middle of the room in the bay window and Nicky had put up tinsel and other decorations around the place. She had also wrapped up all the pictures to make them look like Christmas presents which had a great effect on the look of the rooms. She also got a spray bottle which she normally used for hair and Lauren's hair and filled it with water and put it somewhere handy.

"What's that for?" Richard asked.

"That's for the cat, he goes a bit loopy with trees" Nicky informed him.

Loopy was no exaggeration as at that moment the cat tried to scale the tree and kill it like it was some sort of animal, he was met by a jet of water in the face and he ran away from the tree. Richard was a bit concerned how one can spray water on Christmas lights for them not to blow up but it must be a tried and tested thing by now he thought. When the house was finished it had been totally transformed and it felt so homely and warming to sit relax in it, it really did feel Christmassy and it got Richard thinking about Nicky's face of surprise to see an engagement ring on Christmas morning if he goes ahead with his plan.

Although on the surface things seemed ok, things were starting to crack around the edges. They had not solved the question over what they are going to do about Nicky being pregnant. It seemed as each day went past, Nicky was pushing Richard further and further away from her. Her friend Lisa called around, it's the first time Richard had seen her even though he had been there in Canada about six weeks. Lisa and Nicky decide they are going out on Friday. "Am I going to sit here on my own on a Friday night doing nothing while she goes out partying!?" he thought to himself. It's not that he was against her spending time with her friends, it just felt to him at the time that it was a case she was doing it to spite him, last night she had asked him to sleep on the sofa which he was not altogether happy about. He gave up everything, absolutely everything to come over here to be with her and he done all that, for her now to be pushing him away. And he knows it was because she was pregnant and because of her ex and school it has made things so bad when things had been so good. He didn't know what to do anymore. I know, he thought, I'll email Rachel back in the UK and ask her opinion of everything that's going on.

From: Rich> richard@mynl.com
Sent: 15 December
To: Rachel> rachel@mynl.com
Hi Rachel
I need some advice here, listen I found out some shit...Nicky is pregnant, well first thing is she's not keeping the baby and also I found out she lied to me about breaking up with Jacob when me and her got back together...instead she strung the two of us along till September....please I need your advice.....I know you don't know her or anything but please advise me about how

you think I will take this don't just email me back saying come home....miss ya xxxx
From: Rachel> Rachel@mynl.com
Sent: 16 December
To: Rich> Richard@mynl.com
I'm sorry Rich I really am but I still think she's a bitch and like said before if I ever have the chance to get my hands on her I will kick the shit out of her she's a HEAD FUCK end of...she's selfish and like I also said before it was novelty thing some strange Irish guy coming half way across the world to see her, she likes the attention I told you this and now it looks like I was right and I know you said not to say it BUT PLEASEEEEEEEEEEEEEEEEEE COME HOME PLEASE WE ALL MISS YOU ALL THE PEOPLE THAT REALLY LOVE YOU AND CARE ABOUT YOUR LIFE AND FEELINGS just come home please I'll help you through it I promise x

He didn't want to go along with what Rachel was advising; He was not ready to give up on this. It was nice to have some reassurance from Rachel that she will be there for him if he needs her. Things had been not great between the two of them as she wasn't happy that he had moved off to Canada. Ok so one problem at a time. What does he want to do Friday? He thought to himself 'I think that I want to go out and have fun to take my mind of all the things going on but I need people to go with so I don't sit in the pub by myself.' He logged onto Nicky's laptop and searched some social networks for some local people and got talking to one girl and told her the basics, which is that he's over here from Ireland and having problems with the girlfriend and he just needs a night out but doesn't want to head out alone. She offered for him to meet up with her and her friends, this was good, just what he needed. Friday came and he headed out about half hour after Nicky. When he got to the bar it was empty and so he ordered a couple of drinks to keep himself occupied and then that girl turned up with her friends and he went over and said hello and introduced himself, it wasn't a thing where he or this girl had any sort of interest in each other, to be honest he spent most of the night out on the balcony with her mates having a laugh. He was on vodka and so he was introducing himself to absolutely everyone, the whole town would probably know him after this night. By some strange co-incidence Rachel's band was playing in Herman's that night so he went over and talked to her for a while too. Richard went back to the bar and unsurprisingly Nicky came in with Lisa, he goes over and says hi and said who he was there with, though I think she was too drunk at that point to even hear what he was saying. So he went back over to the people he was with and carried on having a laugh. He did notice Nicky was on the dance floor and stuff but they didn't stay long, probably because he was there. Rachel's band was really good, totally different music to what she played at the singer song writer night. When the club closed in the early hours of the morning Rachel and her friends invited Richard back to the house for a house party, he didn't want to go home yet so he went with them. Their apartment was huge and had a balcony and things, the party consisted of a gang of people all having lots and lots of alcohol and sat around taking turns on the guitar singing songs. That was about it and around eight in the morning he heads home to a very grumpy Nicky, I don't think she appreciated him staying out all night; he plonked himself on the sofa and went to sleep.

When he woke up, Nicky was already awake and sitting on the other sofa having a smoke; she frowned at him when he said good morning.

"You're not annoyed I was out all night are you?" he asks.

"No I don't care" she replied.

After her smoke Nicky runs around getting dressed, Richard puts the bed stuff back in the bedroom and sits on the edge of the bed thinking about things.

"Lisa is here, we always go out for a coffee after a night out, see you later" Nicky said.

"Ok see you later" he replied but was replying to a front door as it closed. When Nicky got back she wanted to talk with him. She wants to make another go of things. He is glad to hear it although if things don't work she wants Richard to go back to Ireland on the 11th of January, which is the date on the return ticket he had bought (which he had planned to change to a later date and had just picked that random date when he had booked the ticket). Nicky seemed angry with him that he had let her carry on drinking and smoking weed knowing that she was pregnant, well yes in the weeks leading up to them finding out she was pregnant they had a lot of alcohol and weed, but they definitely cut down afterwards and he thought he didn't do any encouragement, and he didn't force her to do anything, In fact he is a firm believer that people are in charge of their own actions. Richard had taken it that she doesn't want the baby and so why should he try stop her from drinking if she is not keeping it. Richard is by no means perfect but he gets a lot worse in situations where he is stressed. And now it had come to either things work or he has to go home. Nicky can act ways and blame him for it, and continues to keep him at a distance. If they lived in the same country originally this could have been solved with a bit of space apart to think, but Richard had nowhere else to go and it did hurt. It hurt because he had given up so much, just for Nicky to push him away. He decides to go for a walk and head off down to the boardwalk. His head was rushing, his thoughts were bouncing and his emotions were all over the place. Despite everything he knows he loves Nicky with all his heart, but he also knows that much more of this and he will just break, but if he goes home to Ireland that would break him too. He was in a loose-loose situation and he couldn't see a way out, and he couldn't accept that Nicky wanted to get rid of the baby, it went against everything he believes in, and he no longer felt he had the strength to change her mind about things despite their chat this afternoon, the chat seemed centred on the fact of him going home, and that's something that made him panic. If she wants him to go home sure he might as well go now, but he loves her too much to leave because he knows it will tear his heart out to go. When he gets back from his walk he has made a provisional plan, he sends an email to Rachel in England. He had decided that either way Nicky had settled on the fact that things are coming to an end and now he had to accept that so he can at least be somewhat prepared for what lies ahead.

From: Rich> richard@mynl.com
Sent: 20 Dec
To: Rachel> rachel@mynl.com
Hey
there's a lot going on....but it all came to me and I understand everything that is happening and I have made a plan....it's been some very tough times here but it doesn't bother me now...I am doing ok....sleeping on the sofa.....Nicky thinks we are giving it all another try....she promised to leave all her thoughts out of the way and give me a chance...but you know me I trust more in my instincts.....I think I'll leave next Saturday...travelling on new year's eve arriving Dublin new year's day....with it maybe symbolizing a new start...and that's what I am planning however I am not telling Nicky she will pretend that it doesn't hurt and that will hurt me more than anything.... her kids will probably be in tears because we have got close....I know that....that is how it goes for now....I guess I'll be seeing you soon...I have a tough ten days ahead though I do plan to party it up before I leave.... fuck I'm Irish eh....I need to.

Missing ya
will need a shoulder buddy? Your sofa free?
Rich

The kids came home that evening and it sorted out the atmosphere for a while, well until they had gone to bed anyways. A fight flared up between Richard and Nicky that night. Neither of them could take the situation anymore. He was angry that she wanted to get rid of the baby, she was angry about their night out on town (which Richard didn't know about) and she was angry that she had got pregnant and it all came to a head when he insulted her

"You may study psychology but you sure don't know anything about understanding people" he said and regretted it before the words came off his tongue.

"Get out, take your stuff and leave" she said and their eyes met, their eyes stared at each other as their insides broke. Richard grabs his suitcases from the cupboard and packs everything in a rush, upset because he knows he loves Nicky and he knows she loves him, but he can't force her into this if she has turned her back on things, and he felt bad for the kids who probably heard the very vocal language from the fight and whom would get up in the morning with Richard just vanished, and he did love those kids too, they had really grown on him. He phones for a taxi and leaves, taking a look back at the house Nicky is stood on the doorstep. Deep down she wants to say don't go, deep down she wants to say I love you, but she doesn't. He gets the taxi down to Rachel and Richards house, to be honest it's the only place or option he has, they are good enough to let him sleep on the sofa for the night. "Sleep" well it was more like crying into the pillow for hours before getting a little sleep. Rachel wakes him up and he has to go to work with her as obviously he can't stay there when no one is there. And of course she works with Ethan and that was the last person he wanted to see on that particular morning. So here he found himself at Ethan's place.

"What's going on with you and Nicky eh? I heard you had a fight last night" Ethan asked him as he walked in.

"Yea we had a fight" Richard replied. He had no mental energy not to tell Ethan the truth and he didn't want Ethan breathing down his neck over everything.

"She's pregnant and doesn't want to keep it and I can't cope with that, I want her to keep it" Richard informs Ethan.

Ethan doesn't ask anymore after that and lets Richard go to make some calls upstairs. Richard calls the airline

"Hello can you tell me how much a ticket is from here to Halifax?" he asks.

His ticket only goes from Halifax to Dublin. He doesn't get many straight answers and they are kicking up about him changing his ticket and things but one girl gives him the advice that the best thing to do is just to head to the airport and then he would get sorted out for sure. Thomas had been working away in the basement and Richard goes down to talk to him.

"Thomas, can you take me out to the airport?" Richard asks politely, knowing this is Nicky's family.

"Sure when do you need to go?" he asks in reply.

"Well, as soon as possible I think, I can't be around here anymore" Richard says. They leave and head around to Julia's house.

"What's going on? Julia asks when they arrive.

"Nicky and I had a fight last night...... I'm going to head home." He says.

"But why, you two are great together!? Have you spoken to her today? She asks.

"No but... but she had talked to Ethan and it sounded like she doesn't want me back so..." Richard says with his voice trembling, in fact his hands were trembling too; he was in emotional shock that he was heading home. Thomas lights up a joint and has a bit and makes Richard smoke the rest of it, he doesn't want any emotional chats on the way to the airport and wants to numb things down for Richard seeing him in a state; maybe he's like a doctor or something. Before Richard knew it he was super stoned. Thomas drives Richard out to the airport, Richard thought a lot about Nicky, and thought a lot about the kids, and he didn't think Nicky will miss him but that the kids would.

"Hey would you do me a favour Thomas? Can you say goodbye to the kids for me?" He says.

"Yea I will" Thomas says. Thomas drops Richard off at the airport which is about half hour from town.

Nicky woke up and made coffee and sat on the back step having a smoke. The kids are awake and wanting to see her and maybe ask her questions, she holds the door handle, doesn't want to deal with them yet. Finally she opens the door and answers the questions.

"Where's Richard gone?"

"He's left he's gone" she told them. Nicky rings her dad and tells him what's gone on and that she had a fight with Richard and he's gone somewhere. Thomas calls by later to see if she is ok.

"Hey what's up girl, I heard you and Richard had a big fight, are you ok?" he asks

"Yea I'm ok; do you know where he is?" she asked him.

"I'm just after dropping him to the airport, he's headed back to Ireland" he tells her.

"What?" she says in disbelief. The situation suddenly hit her. She might have had a fight, but she didn't want him to head to Ireland, she didn't even want him to leave, and now he's gone and everything is lost.

It's Christmas day and Richard opens his eyes, he is laying in the spare bed at Rachel's house in England. He couldn't make it all the way home to Ireland because all the flights were fully booked with the time of year that it was, but a stay at his best friend's house is probably what he needed anyway. He sat up on the bed still in his clothes from the day before, there on the floor is the remnants of the night before, a half empty can of cider. He picks it up and starts drinking, and follows the stairs down. Everyone in the house is up and some presents are shared around. Rachel in short notice had bought him some socks. Rachel and her family go out visiting later in the day and Richard goes for a walk. He walks down to the park, walking through the trees in the cold winter air. He thinks about all that has happened, he thinks about all he has lost. He looks deep inside himself and does not see much hope in fact he sees none. This was the day he was going to propose and it's all gone and he's all alone. He sits down beside a tree, and considers never returning, never returning anywhere, he doesn't deserve to see Ria, and feels a burden to his friends here in England. His thoughts rush like a flood bursting the banks of a river and tears begin to stroll down his face. He knows he still loves Nicky and can't bear to be without her in his life, and so for a while he sits there considering putting an end to it, and end to the empty life he feels he now has. The tears outnumber the thoughts and he calms down a bit and heads back to the house to get drunk.

It's early January and Nicky is lying on a clinic table in Halifax, she had travelled there with her dad. This was a day she had dreaded for a long time. Even though she had told Richard she wanted to get rid of the baby, she knew deep down she didn't want to do such a thing, she was just scared. Looking at that ultrasound screen she seen the baby moving inside of her and could hear the little heart beat, the nurse hands her a picture. It's all too much for her and she puts her hand to her face to hide her eyes, as her eyes would tell a story to the nurse, the story of a broken heart and an angry mind. Why didn't Richard stop her drinking? How could he disappear on me and leave me like this? Maybe he's gone back and has forgotten everything and he doesn't care. She didn't want to cry. She hates crying however she can't stop that tear rolling down her face. Deep down she still loves him and misses him and wishes that on that fateful night that when Richard was climbing into that taxi that her heart had told her mouth to say the words don't go, but right now, right now at this moment she hated him. She hated him that he had gone and she hated him that she had to say goodbye to the baby inside of her.

About the Author

Charlie is a young writer who seems to soak up how people are. Almost like a sponge she will absorb stories and experiences of human nature. Through this she hopes to tell stories which stay true to real life experiences in this modern world. Charlie also studies body language and psychology to understand how a person's movement and decisions are a complex result of a person's past.